BY ORDER OF THE SECRETARY
OF THE AIR FORCE

AIR FORCE MANUAL 15-111

27 FEBRUARY 2013

Weather

SURFACE WEATHER OBSERVATIONS

COMPLIANCE WITH THIS PUBLICATION IS MANDATORY

ACCESSIBILITY: This publication is available for downloading from the e-publishing website at www.e-publishing.af.mil

RELEASABILITY: There are no releasability restrictions on this publication

OPR: HQ USAF/A3O-WP

Supersedes: AFMAN 15-111,
        10 March 2009

Certified by: HQ USAF/A3O-W
(Dr. Fred P. Lewis)
Pages: 118

This manual implements Air Force Policy Directive (AFPD) 15-1, *Atmospheric and Space Environmental Support*. It also implements Federal Meteorological Handbook No. 1 (FCM-H1) and the World Meteorological Organization (WMO) Manual on Codes, Volume I.1, Part A (WMO 306, Vol I.1, Part A) aerodrome routine meteorological reports (FM-15 METAR) and aerodrome special meteorological reports (FM-16 SPECI) codes. It prescribes basic observing fundamentals and terms and establishes aviation code forms for recording and disseminating weather observations. It applies to all Active and Reserve Component organizations conducting weather operations, including government-contracted weather operations if stated in the Statement of Work or Performance Work Statement. This Air Force (AF) Manual (AFMAN) may be supplemented at any level, but all supplements must be routed to AF/A3O-WP, 1490 Air Force Pentagon, Washington, DC 20330-1490 for coordination prior to certification and approval. Refer recommended changes and questions about this publication to AF/A3O-WP using the AF 847, *Recommendation for Change of Publication*; route AF 847s from the field through Major Command (MAJCOM) publications/forms managers. Ensure that all records created as a result of processes prescribed in this publication are maintained in accordance with AFMAN 33-363, *Management of Records*, and disposed of in accordance with the Air Force Records Disposition Schedule (RDS) located in the Air Force Records Information Management System (AFRIMS). The use of the name or mark of any specific manufacturer, commercial product, commodity or service in this publication does not imply endorsement by the Air Force.

SUMMARY OF CHANGES

This revision substantially reorganizes and streamlines weather observing practices within Air Force weather. Included are policies requiring full automation of weather observing systems and procedures for augmenting automated meteorological observing systems. Many legacy practices and systems, including earthquake reporting, nuclear accident reporting, ML-102 aneroid barometer, and Digital Barometer and Altimeter Setting Indicator have been deleted.

Chapter 1

INTRODUCTION

1.1. Background Information. This manual prescribes AF METAR weather observing and reporting procedures based on agreements with the WMO, the International Civil Aviation Organization (ICAO), National Weather Service (NWS), Federal Aviation Administration (FAA), international and domestic aviation interests and other civil weather services.

1.2. General. FCM-H1 establishes standard United States (US) surface weather observation requirements and procedures for US Federal meteorological agencies. Based on FCM-H1, this manual incorporates procedures applicable to AF weather operations in both US and overseas locations. Visibility values are reported in statute miles at US locations (including Hawaii, Alaska and Guam); at OCONUS locations visibility values are reported in the same units as the visibility minimums published for the installation in the DoD FLIPs.

1.3. Applicability of Procedures. The procedures in this manual apply to all AF and Army weather organizations performing automated, manual or augmented observing operations. No set of procedures can cover all possibilities in weather observing. Weather technicians must use their own judgment, adhering as closely as possible to the procedures in this manual, to describe phenomena not covered adequately by this publication.

Chapter 2

GENERAL OBSERVING INFORMATION

2.1. General. This chapter contains general procedures pertaining to all AF weather organizations responsible for providing and/or arranging for surface weather observations.

2.1.1. Airfield services functions, weather flights, operating locations, and detachments will be referred to in this document as exploitation units (EU).

2.1.2. The EU will function as the "eyes forward" for the servicing operational weather squadron (OWS), and in many cases, will serve as the primary point of contact for the collaborative forecast effort to include resource protection for the installation.

2.1.3. The responsibilities of EUs are outlined in Air Force Instruction (AFI) 15-128, *Air Force Weather Roles and Responsibilities* and AFMAN 15-129, Volume 2, *Air and Space Weather Operations - Exploitation.*

2.2. Automated Meteorological Observing Systems (AMOS). An AMOS refers to any certified AF owned and AF or Army certified observing system (e.g., AN/FMQ-19, AN/TMQ-53, Automated Surface Observing System (ASOS)) with the capability to automatically collect and disseminate observations.

2.2.1. AMOSs will be operated in full automated mode, at Department of Defense (DoD) controlled airfields, to provide the official METAR and SPECI observations, **except** under the conditions specified in 3.2.1. EU leadership, after formal coordination with supported AF or Army organization leadership, will develop procedures based on sound Operational Risk Management (ORM) practices to ensure weather technicians are readily available to supplement and/or back-up observations as required in Chapter 3.

2.2.2. In the automated mode, the system continually senses and measures the atmosphere for the following weather elements and parameters: Wind, Visibility, Precipitation/Obstructions to Vision, Cloud Height, Sky Cover, Temperature, Dew Point, Altimeter, and Lightning. The system will report wind speed and direction, visibility, thunderstorms, precipitation, obscurations to visibility, cloud height, sky cover, temperature, dew point and altimeter setting on all observations. The system will also format and report specific automated remarks as detailed in Attachment 3.

2.2.3. Automated stations will always be considered automated, even when a weather technician augments or backs up an observation.

2.2.4. Non-AF or non- Army controlled airfields (i.e., those not owned and operated by US military authorities) may be supported by AMOSs. There are many locations to include ranges, training areas, drop zones, military operation areas, and uncontrolled airfields where AMOSs provide stand-alone weather information.

2.2.5. Organizations will update Flight Information Publication (FLIP) references IAW AFI 11-201, *Flight Information Publications,* to specify those DoD controlled airfields operating with an AMOS. Detailed procedures on updating FLIPs can be found at **https://weather.af.mil/confluence/display/AFPUBLIC/Weather+Techniques+and+Procedures** #.

2.3. Fixed Meteorological Equipment. The following requirements apply to all primary meteorological equipment used in the generation of surface weather observations at both automated and augmented weather observing locations.

2.3.1. Equipment Maintenance, Calibration, and Standardization. EUs will perform required user/operator maintenance IAW equipment Technical Orders (TOs)/operator manuals. EUs will also ensure host/supporting airfield systems and computer maintenance personnel provide maintenance to meteorological and communications systems, to include equipment calibration and standardization IAW established maintenance schedules and other contract or local instructions outlining acceptable maintenance support and response times. Calibration and standardization should be performed upon installation and at least annually thereafter, and after any major maintenance is performed on an instrument or sensor.

2.3.2. Siting and Exposure. As best as practical, AMOS sensor groups will be sited IAW the FCM-S4-1994, *Federal Standard for Siting Meteorological Sensors at Airports*. Currently installed sensors may be operated at their present locations. However, if they are relocated, the federal standards will be followed. EUs will coordinate with the host/supporting airfield systems maintenance to perform an annual inspection of all meteorological equipment and ensure equipment is in good condition and verify no obstructions are affecting the equipment's siting and exposure. EU leadership should accompany maintenance personnel on this inspection and log any new equipment limitation(s) into appropriate Flight Information Handbook or report equipment issues to higher level(s) (e.g., AFWA, MAJCOM).

2.3.3. AMOSs will be certified IAW the *Air Force Weather Station Certification & Observing System 21st Century (OS-21) Commissioning Plan*. This document identifies the process EUs will use to certify AMOSs at Air Force and Army sites. The commissioning plan is located at https://weather.af.mil/confluence/download/attachments/10846889/Wx_Station_Certification_and_OS21_Commissioning_Plan.pdf.

2.4. Certification Requirements.

2.4.1. Weather technicians will be fully trained, task certified, and position qualified according to requirements outlined in AFI 15-127, Air Force Weather Qualification Training and local training requirements.

2.4.2. Weather technicians will task-certify ATC personnel to evaluate prevailing visibility values from the control tower. If required, weather technicians will also ensure ATC personnel can operate the applicable weather equipment in ATC facilities. Log ATC task certification on ATC provided AF 3622, *Air Traffic Control/Weather Certification and Rating Record*.

2.5. Station Information File. EUs responsible for preparing surface weather observations, regardless of the mode of operation, will ensure their station information is current and maintained on permanent file at the 14th Weather Squadron (14WS) and in the observing locations historical file. See **Attachment 4** for a list of information required. E-mail information to the 14WS at "14WS customersvc@afccc.af.mil" and 2SYOS/SYSD at "2SOS/SYSD@offutt.af.mil" or mail it to:

14WS/WXD
151 Patton Avenue
Asheville, NC 28801-5002

and

2SYOS/SYSD
101 Nelson Dr
Offutt AFB, NE 68113-1023

Note: E-mail addresses may change without notice.

2.6. Accuracy of Time. The accuracy of the time ascribed to weather observations is of the utmost importance, especially in aviation safety investigations.

2.6.1. EUs will designate a single timepiece as the standard clock and establish procedures to perform a time check on a daily basis. The standard clock will be a standalone clock zeroed with the US Naval Observatory time. A synchronized computer network clock may be used as the standard clock if it is verified that the Base/Post network time is synchronized on a daily basis with a Global Positioning System or US Naval Observatory clock. Annotate a time check in Column 90 on either AF 3803/3813, as applicable.

2.6.2. Adjust internal clocks of all applicable equipment (e.g., Joint Environmental Toolkit (JET), AN/FMQ-19) to the time of the standard clock with each accomplished time check. Record any time corrections to equipment in Column 90, (e.g., 0605 ADS CLOCK ADJUSTED +20 SECONDS).

2.7. Aviation Weather Code Forms. In addition to prescribing basic observing fundamentals and terms, this manual establishes aviation code forms for recording and disseminating METAR, SPECI, and LOCAL weather observations.

2.7.1. Aviation Routine Weather Report (METAR). METAR is a routine scheduled observation as well as the primary observation code used by the United States to satisfy requirements for reporting surface meteorological data. METAR contains a complete report of wind, visibility, runway visual range, present weather and obscurations, sky condition, temperature, dew point and altimeter setting collectively referred to as "the body of the report." In addition, encoded and/or plain language information that elaborates on data in the body of the report may be appended to the METAR. The contents of the remarks will vary according to the mode of operation (e.g., automated or augmented), and are defined in each part of this manual.

2.7.1.1. EUs will establish METAR file times between H+55 to H+59 minutes past the hour. When augmenting an AMOS, the last observed element is the ascribed time of the observation to the nearest minute H+55 to H+59.

2.7.1.2. METAR observations taken at 0000, 0600, 1200, and 1800 UTC include additional data and are known as 6-hourly observations. The METAR observations taken at 0300, 0900, 1500, and 2100 UTC are known as 3-hourly observations and also contain additional information.

2.7.2. Aviation Selected Special Weather Report (SPECI).   SPECI is an unscheduled observation completed and transmitted when any of the special criteria listed in **Attachment 2** are observed or sensed.   SPECI will contain all data elements found in a METAR plus additional remarks that elaborate on data in the body of the report.   All SPECI reports will be prepared and transmitted as soon as possible after the relevant criteria are observed.

2.7.2.1. The time ascribed to a SPECI reflects the time, to the nearest minute, that the SPECI criteria are first met or observed. For a METAR with SPECI criteria, the actual time of the observation will be H+55 to H+59 minutes past the hour (standard time of a METAR observation).

2.7.2.2. Range criteria may take the place of the criteria in **Attachment 2**.

2.7.2.3. COCOM/MAJCOM or higher headquarters may replace the criteria values in **Attachment 2** with values from Combatant Commander instructions, manuals or supplements relating to command minima for landing, visual flight rules (VFR), instrument flight rules (IFR) and alternates.

2.7.3. Aviation Selected Local Weather Report (LOCAL).   A LOCAL is an unscheduled observation, reported to the nearest minute, not meeting SPECI criteria. LOCALs will only be taken when local leadership determines there is a requirement in support of local operations or OPSEC considerations.   For LOCALs taken in support of aircraft operations, the code form will be METAR.   For LOCALs taken and disseminated to other than ATC agencies, the contents may be established locally and specified in base/host unit plans, local weather support agreements or standard operating procedures.   LOCAL altimeter setting observations are taken at an interval not to exceed 35 minutes when there has been a change of 0.01 inch Hg (0.3 hPa) or more since the last ALSTG value. A METAR or SPECI taken within the established time interval will meet this requirement. All LOCAL altimeter setting reports will be prepared and disseminated as soon as possible after the relevant altimeter setting change is observed.

2.8. Observed Elements.

2.8.1. Automated Observations.   AMOSs use time averaging of sensor data.   In an automated observation, sky condition will be an evaluation of sensor data gathered during the 30-minute period ending at the actual time of the observation. All other elements evaluated are based on sensor data that is within 10 minutes or less of the actual time of the observation.   For the "objective" element; such as pressure, temperature, dew point, and wind; automated and augmented observations use a fixed location and time-averaging technique.   For the "subjective" elements; such as sky condition, visibility, and present weather; augmented observations use a fixed time, spatial averaging technique to describe the visual elements, while an AMOS will use a fixed location, time-linear technique. Some AMOSs are capable of generating an observation every minute.   The One-Minute Observation (OMO) is encoded in METAR format and includes all basic weather parameters found in the body of the METAR plus specific automated remarks. The OMO also accepts augmented elements and remarks.   The difference between the OMO and the METAR/SPECI is that the OMO is not disseminated. The weather technician can manually disseminate the OMO if required, for example, upon arrival at an Alternate Operating Location (AOL).

2.8.2. Augmented Observations. Individual elements entered in an observation must, as closely as possible, reflect conditions existing at the actual time of observation. Elements entered will have been observed within 15 minutes of the actual time of the observation. Gusts and squalls will be reported if observed within 10 minutes of the actual time of the observation. Observation of elements will be made as close to the scheduled time of the observation as possible to meet filing deadlines, but in no case will these observations be started more than 15 minutes before the scheduled time. Supplement elements evaluated instrumentally with visual observations to ensure accuracy.

2.8.2.1. Order of Observing. Elements having the greatest rate of change are evaluated last. When conditions are relatively unchanging, evaluate the elements in the following order:

2.8.2.1.1. Elements evaluated outdoors. Before taking observations at night, spend as much time as practicable outside to allow your eyes to become adjusted to the limited light of the nighttime sky.

2.8.2.1.2. Elements evaluated indoors, with pressure last.

2.9. Installation Observation Requirements.

2.9.1. At all EUs, the local ceiling, prevailing visibility, and runway visual range landing and circling minima will be SPECI observations generated by the AMOS or the weather technician. SPECI criteria will be based on published airfield minima (take-off, landing, circling) for all approaches (e.g., Instrument Landing System (ILS), Tactical Air Navigation system (TACAN)) and other AF, higher headquarters, MAJCOM, Army and installation directives. EUs with an AMOS will update SPECI criteria in the software to ensure the system generates the required SPECI observations.

2.9.2. Flight Information Publication (FLIP) Review. EUs will have procedures to review each new edition of DoD FLIPs, including the Radar Instrument Approach Minimums, local NOTAMs and applicable directives for changes in the airfield minima as soon as possible after publication. See the Air Force Weather Techniques and Procedures – Flight Information Publication Procedures located at **https://weather.af.mil/confluence/download/attachments/12653971/Weather_Technique s_and_Procedures_3.2.1._FLIP_Procedures.pdf**.

2.9.3. Magnetic Variation. The local magnetic variation must be determined at each observing location to convert wind direction from magnetic to true. Obtain local magnetic variation from the installations DoD FLIPs or the Tactical Plotting Chart for your area, whichever is most current, or the National Oceanographic Atmospheric Association National Geophysical Data Center website located at **http://www.ngdc.noaa.gov/geomag-web/#declination**. Local variation will change by several minutes of arc each year at most locations. Weather leadership must monitor FLIPS or revised charts for changes in local magnetic direction. Shifts in variation may affect the orientation of the wind equipment; therefore, keep maintenance personnel informed of changes.

2.9.3.1. From magnetic to true: (1) add easterly variation to magnetic direction, and (2) subtract westerly variation from magnetic direction.

2.9.3.2. From true to magnetic: (1) add westerly variation to true direction, and (2) subtract easterly variation from true direction.

2.10. Unofficial Weather Reports. Unofficial weather reports are defined as a report of one or more weather elements from an individual who is not task certified to take official weather observations (e.g., a pilot or law enforcement official). Unofficial reports can provide additional and supplemental information that may be important to local aviation and public safety. It can also help increase the weather technician's situational awareness. Unofficial reports of severe weather from credible sources within 15 statute miles will be appended in the remarks of the observation and disseminated longline and locally during augmentation of an AMOS (e.g., unconfirmed tornado 9 statute miles west of KFAW per law enforcement). Follow up credible reports of severe weather with the supporting OWS. Mission-restricting weather may be appended in the remarks of the observation and sent out at the technician's discretion.

2.11. Points of Observation. For meteorological observations, the observing location is defined as the "Point of Observation." "Points of Observation" are locations where the various elements of the observation are evaluated. Normally, these locations are confined to an area within 5 statute miles (8000 meters) of the runway complex, drop zone, or landing zone. In cases where all measurements are taken at approximately the same point, a weather organization will be regarded as having a single observation location. In cases where various sensors are in different locations to obtain acceptable exposure, the weather observations may also contain information on phenomena occurring at areas other than the official observing location (e.g., clouds over mountains W, lightning SE, thunderstorms NW). However, in such cases, the point of observation is not extended to include points where the distant phenomena are occurring. For example, at a large, modern airfield, the points of observation are generally considered as follows:

2.11.1. Automated Observations: The location of the primary sensor group and the discontinuity sensor group. The latitude, longitude, and elevation information should be provided to the supporting OWS and forwarded to the Air Force Weather Agency (AFWA) if the instrumentation is moved or a site survey shows the reported information to be in error.

2.11.2. Augmented Observations:

2.11.2.1. For elements such as prevailing visibility, present weather, obscurations and all cloud height and ceiling elements, the observing location may be coincident with the weather observing location; or it may be the touchdown area of the primary runway. The selected location must provide consistent visually determined values.

2.11.2.2. The center of the runway complex for temperature, dew point, pressure, lightning and winds if the sensor is not installed at touchdown areas. If there is no sensing capability available on the runway complex, weather technicians may obtain temperature, dew point, pressure, lightning and wind data using back-up methods at the observing location.

2.11.2.3. A point near the approach end of a runway for touchdown runway visual range (RVR) and winds.

2.12. Rounding of Figures and Values. Except where otherwise designated, round figures and values as follows:

2.12.1. If the fractional part of a positive number to be dropped is equal to or greater than one-half, the preceding digit will be increased by one. If the fractional part of a negative number to be dropped is greater than one-half, the preceding digit will be decreased by one. In all other cases, the preceding digit will remain unchanged. For example, 1.5 becomes 2, -1.5 becomes -1, 1.3 becomes 1, and -2.6 becomes -3.

2.12.2. When cloud height and visibility values are halfway or less between two reportable values, report the lower value. For example, cloud heights of 2,549 feet and 2,550 feet are reported as 2,500 feet, visibility values of 5 1/4 statute miles (8250 meters) and 5 1/2 statute miles (8500 meters) are reported as 5 statute miles (8000 meters).

2.12.3. When cloud height and visibility values are greater than halfway between two reportable values, report the higher value. For example, a cloud height of 2,451 feet is reported as 2,500 feet, and a visibility value of 4 3/4 statute miles (7750 meters) is reported as 5 statute miles (8000 meters).

2.12.4. When computations of pressure values require that a number be rounded to comply with standards on reportable values, the number will be rounded down to the next reportable value. For example, a station pressure reading of 29.249 is rounded down to 29.245 while a station pressure reading of 29.244 is rounded down to 29.240. Altimeter setting readings of 29.249 and 29.244 are both truncated to 29.24.

2.12.5. Altimeter settings provided for international aviation purposes and reported in whole hectopascals (hPa) are rounded down when disposing of tenths of hPa (e.g., 1009.9 hPa and 1009.1 hPa are both rounded down to 1009 hPa).

2.13. Alternate Operating Location (AOL). EUs responsible for preparing surface weather observations, without regard to the mode of operation, will establish an AOL when the primary location is evacuated. EUs will work with the local command to establish an AOL and outline what is needed from various agencies on the installation to support operations at the location. Operations at the AOL and any reciprocal support from other agencies will be coordinated and formally documented in base/host unit plans or a local weather support document. See AFMAN 15-129, Volume 2, *Air Force Weather Operations - Exploitation*, for additional guidance on operating at an AOL.

2.13.1. The AOL will be a location with adequate communications and a view of the airfield complex. Some EUs may be equipped to augment the AMOS at the AOL, assuming the AMOS sensors are still working. If the sensors are not operating, or there is no interface available to augment the AMOS, EUs should plan to use available back-up equipment (e.g., deployable equipment) and methods to prepare the observation.

2.13.2. Within 15 minutes of arrival at the AOL, weather technicians will complete and transmit an augmented observation. The "eyes forward" function will begin as soon as practical after the observation is transmitted. **Note:** Observation is not required at automated locations if AMOS is working properly and no mandatory supplementary criteria are occurring.

2.13.3. At a minimum, weather technicians must be able to prepare an initial observation containing the minimum required elements (i.e., wind speed and direction, prevailing visibility, present weather and obscurations, sky condition, temperature, dew point and altimeter setting). Mandatory elements may be omitted from the observation if the necessary equipment is not available.

2.13.4. Resume normal observing operations (i.e., automated, augmented) upon return to the primary observing location.

2.14. Weather Watch. Weather technicians at augmented EUs will perform one of two types of weather watch: a Basic Weather Watch (BWW), or a Continuous Weather Watch (CWW). **Note:** At automated locations, the AMOS performs an automatic CWW. When augmentation is required, weather personnel will perform the BWW (EUs may also perform a CWW if locally determined to be more appropriate due to existing meteorological conditions).

2.14.1. Basic Weather Watch. A BWW will be conducted when the airfield is open and during periods when any of the mandatory augmentation of AMOS is required IAW Chapter 3. Due to these other weather duties, weather technicians on duty may not detect and report all weather changes as they occur. During a BWW, weather technicians will recheck weather conditions, at intervals not to exceed 20 minutes since the last observation/recheck, to determine the need for a SPECI observation, when any of the following conditions are observed to be occurring or are forecast to occur within 1 hour:

2.14.1.1. Ceiling forms below or decreases to less than 1,500 feet.

2.14.1.2. Ceiling dissipates, or increases to equal or exceed 1,500 feet.

2.14.1.3. Visibility decreases to less than 3 statute miles (4800 meters).

2.14.1.4. Visibility increases to equal or exceed 3 statute miles (4800 meters).

2.14.1.5. Precipitation (any form).

2.14.1.6. Thunderstorms

2.14.1.7. Fog or Mist.

2.14.1.8. All supplemental criteria specified in Table 3.1.

2.14.1.9. During mandatory back-up of AMOS IAW Para 3.4.

2.14.1.10. In addition to the above minimum requirements, weather technicians will remain alert for any other changes in weather conditions that will require a SPECI observation. Weather technicians will also monitor local area observational and forecast products as often as necessary to keep abreast of changes expected to affect their area of responsibility.

2.14.2. Continuous Weather Watch. At augmented EUs that require a CWW, weather technicians will monitor weather conditions continuously and perform no other significant duties. In addition to taking METARs, weather technicians will take and disseminate observations as conditions occur that meet SPECI observation criteria. EUs may perform a CWW during AMOS augmentation if locally determined to be more appropriate due to existing meteorological conditions.

2.15. Cooperative Weather Watch. EUs responsible for preparing surface weather observations, without regard to the mode of operation, will establish a cooperative weather watch with ATC and other appropriate base/post agencies, as required. Of primary concern is the report of tower visibility different from the prevailing surface visibility, local PIREPs and any occurrence of previously unreported weather conditions that could affect flight safety or be critical to the safety or efficiency of other local operations and resources. All weather technicians must thoroughly understand and be able to execute every element in the local cooperative weather watch agreement.

2.15.1. The cooperative weather watch will define, at a minimum, the process for task certified ATC personnel to report changes in tower prevailing visibility to the local EU when tower visibility is less than 4 statute miles (6000 meters) and different from the surface prevailing visibility.

2.15.2. As part of the cooperative weather watch, if continuous RVR reporting is needed during airfield closure hours, EUs with AMOS systems will notify airfield leadership that the RVR system requires the runway lights to be left on to work properly. This is encouraged if the possibility exists for an emergency aircraft divert into the location.

2.15.3. EUs will coordinate cooperative weather watch requirements in base/host unit plans or local weather support agreement.

2.16. Control Tower Observations and Weather Observing Location Actions.

2.16.1. ATC Personnel. ATC directives (e.g., AFI 13-204, Volume 3, *Airfield Operations Procedures and Programs*; FAAO JO 7110.65, *Air Traffic Control,* TC 3-04.81 (FM 3-04.303) *Air Traffic Control Facility Operations, Training, Maintenance, and Standardization*) require task certified control tower personnel to make tower prevailing visibility observations when the prevailing visibility at the usual point of observation or at the tower level, is less than 4 statute miles (6000 meters). Control tower personnel task certified to take visibility observations will also notify the weather technician when the observed tower prevailing visibility decreases to less than or increases to equal or exceed 4 statute miles (6000 meters).

2.16.2. Weather technicians at augmented EUs will:

2.16.2.1. Notify the tower, as soon as possible, whenever the prevailing visibility at the official weather observation point decreases to less than or increases to equal or exceed 4 statute miles (6000 meters).

2.16.2.2. Re-evaluate surface prevailing visibility, as soon as practicable, upon initial receipt of a differing control tower value and upon receipt of subsequent reportable changes at the control tower level.

2.16.2.3. Use control tower values of prevailing visibility as a guide in determining the surface visibility when the view of portions of the horizon is obstructed by buildings, aircraft, etc. The presence of a surface-based obscuration, uniformly distributed to heights above the level of the tower, is sufficient reason to consider the EUs prevailing visibility the same as the control tower level.

2.17. Observing Aids for Visibility. EUs will post charts, lists or other positive means of identifying lights or objects used as observing aids near the weather technician's position (both primary, alternate observing locations and augment locations for AMOS sites) so they can be accessed quickly and easily. Separate lists or charts may be used for daytime and nighttime markers. In any case, the aids must be clearly identified as to whether they are daytime or nighttime aids. EUs will update visibility charts at least annually.

2.17.1. Observing locations should research the availability of detailed host installation maps/references first and as required submit a work order to survey the markers through the local Base Civil Engineering or Army equivalent (if on an Army installation) agency to create visibility aids/charts. Deployed locations should use available tools, such as military grid reference system maps, laser range finder equipment, and global positioning system devices to determine distances to visibility markers and create visibility aids/charts.

2.17.2. The most suitable daytime markers are prominent dark or nearly dark colored objects (such as buildings, chimneys, hills or trees) observed in silhouette against a light-colored background, preferably the horizon sky. When using an object located in front of a terrestrial background, use caution when the object is located closer to the point of observation than it is to the terrestrial background.

2.17.3. The most desirable night-visibility markers are unfocused lights of moderate intensity (about 25 candelas). The red or green runway course lights of airway beacons and TV or radio tower obstruction lights may be used. Do not use focused lights such as airway beacons due to their intensity; however, their brilliance may serve as an aid in estimating whether the visibility is greater or less than the distance to the light source.

2.17.4. Representative visibility markers should be high quality (color/digital) photos taken on a predominantly cloud and obscuration free (clear) day and be representative of the current state of the airfield/site (see **Figure 2.1**). It is also recommended observing locations develop map-type visibility charts to augment the photographic visibility markers.

Figure 2.1. Example Visibility Checkpoint Photograph

2.17.5. Control Tower Visibility Aids. ATC regulations require control towers to maintain a visibility checkpoint chart or list of visibility markers posted in the tower. Upon request,

EUs will provide whatever assistance is necessary to help prepare a chart or markers of suitable objects for determining tower visibility.

2.18. Aircraft Mishap. Upon notification of an aircraft mishap, EUs will:

2.18.1. Collect and save data related to an aircraft mishap according to instructions in AFMAN 15-129, Volume 2, *Air Force Weather Operations - Exploitation.* Technicians will retrieve the archived surface observation data as required by the requesting agency.

2.18.2. All EUs regardless of operating mode will encode/disseminate a SPECI observation IAW instructions detailed in this document.

2.19. Supplementary Data for an Inactive or Parallel Runway. ATC may occasionally authorize an aircraft to land using an inactive runway. This is a temporary measure and the current (official) observation is not affected since the active runway is not officially changed. However, if weather sensors are installed on the inactive runway, the ATC agency may initiate a requirement for observational data to control aircraft using that runway. At locations where ATC has procedures to land aircraft on an inactive runway, the EU will develop specific procedures coordinated with ATC and specified in the base/host unit plans or a local weather support document. Any requirement must be based on the following factors:

2.19.1. Wind and RVR. These are the only sensor-derived elements likely to differ between the two runways. Current wind data from sensors near the runway are normally available to the controller by means of a switching capability in the tower. Therefore, procedures for supplementary data are generally necessary only for RVR. At augmented locations, if required, RVR for an inactive runway must be reported using the same basic code form as that specified for the active runway (e.g., to include the runway number). Supplemental RVR data can be encoded and transmitted as a remark in column 13. Wind data from dual parallel runways can be reported in the remarks section of a METAR or SPECI observation whenever a 6-knot sustained or gust speed difference exists between the active end wind sensors. Example: WND RWY 32R 300/10G15KT.

2.19.2. Cloud Heights. Cloud heights generally do not differ from one end of a runway to the other. However, AMOS discontinuity sensors will report cloud ceiling heights as a remark in the observation. Any variation in sky condition relative to the runways, such as reported in local PIREPs, can be taken into consideration in the evaluation of sky cover as reported in the official observation. EUs may report in the remarks section of the observation significant or unusual variations in the sky condition (e.g., CLD LYR AT 400 FT ON APCH RWY 23 RPRTD BY PIREPS) that could affect flying operations.

2.20. Instrument Procedures.

2.20.1. When the accuracy or validity of values from meteorological equipment is questionable, discontinue use of such equipment and use back-up equipment and methods until corrective maintenance actions have been accomplished. **Note**: AMOSs obtain data and compute elements differently from manual observing methods. Weather technicians should take into account these differences before logging any system or sensor out.

2.20.2. Dual Instrumentation/Outage. EUs with weather equipment sensors installed near the approach end of two or more runways will use the sensors installed at the active (approach) end of the runway when the equipment is operational and considered reliable. If cloud height equipment for the active runway is inoperative, data obtained from the inactive runway (or alternate runway) equipment may be used if the measurements are considered representative. If wind equipment is inoperative, determine wind data for the runway in use using the most reliable system available (i.e., inactive runway instrumentation, hand-held anemometer, Beaufort scale, etc.) and include a WND DATA ESTMD remark. If the RVR equipment is inoperative and visibility is equal to or less than 1 mile (1600 meters), RVR is reported locally and longline as RVRNO. Do not use the alternate end RVR.

Chapter 3

AUGMENTATION

3.1. Purpose. This chapter describes the procedures to augment surface weather observations produced by an AMOS.

3.2. Augmentation. Augmentation is the process of having position-qualified weather technicians manually add or edit data to an observation generated by a properly sited AMOS. The two augmentation processes used are *supplement* and *back-up*. **Supplementing** is a method of manually adding meteorological information to an automated observation that is beyond the capabilities of the AMOS to detect and/or report. Table 3.1 identifies elements that are mandatory to supplement. **Back-up** is the method of manually providing meteorological data and/or dissemination to an AMOS observation when the primary automated method is not operational or unavailable due to sensor and/or communication failure.

3.2.1. Determining Augmentable Observation Elements. EUs will only augment for those items listed in Table 3.1 and those that would adversely impact flight/ground operations, based on documented supported unit requirements, if not augmented. EUs will use manual observing methods (e.g., prevailing visibility reporting, thunderstorm reporting) when augmenting an AMOS. Back-up the specific observation elements that are missing or incorrect due to sensor and/or communication failure.

3.2.2. Automated Dissemination System (ADS). In this manual, ADS refers to any Air Force, Army or NWS accredited dissemination system (e.g., JET or Advanced Weather Interactive Processing System (AWIPS)).

3.2.3. Augmentation Responsibilities. To perform augmentation duties, the weather technician must maintain situational awareness of current weather conditions and AMOS observations. EUs will develop ORM based augmentation procedures and clearly defined duty priorities that include augmentation. These duties will be coordinated and defined in the local weather support agreement or equivalent document. In all cases, the highest priority will be flight safety.

3.2.4. Entering and Disseminating Augmented Information. EUs will use ADS to enter and disseminate augmented information. If an ADS is not available for use during augmentation, EUs will develop back-up procedures to disseminate locally and use an applicable back-up weather system interface to disseminate longline (e.g., Air Force Weather Web Services (AFW-WEBS)).

3.2.5. Documenting Augmented Observations. EUs will document AMOS augmented observations using ADS (JET) Form 3813, electronic or paper AF 3803, or the approved electronic workbook version (Excel®) of Form 3803 (available: **https://notus2.afccc.af.mil/SCIS/form3803info.asp**).

3.2.6. All AN/TMQ-53s used must be properly set up and sited as best as practical IAW FCM-S4-1994 prior to use in automated mode. Additionally, EUs will not use UTC-postured (deployable) AN/TMQ-53s as their permanent base/post observing system. **Note:** Known limitations on the extended heights of AN/TMQ-53 visibility and wind sensors prevent full compliance with all applicable FSM-S4-1994 sensor siting standards.

3.2.7. ADS Dissemination. Weather technicians should only configure their ADS to disseminate in the "augmented" versus "automated" mode when augmentation is required. Selecting the ADS "augmented" dissemination mode removes the "AUTO" report modifier from the METAR/SPECI observation. When augmentation is no longer required, weather personnel must reconfigure their ADS to disseminate in a fully automated mode to turn on the "AUTO" report modifier.

3.3. Supplementing AMOSs. Weather technicians are required to have a view of the airfield complex when supplementing an AMOS. Weather technicians will perform a BWW and be prepared to supplement observations when the airfield is open and the weather conditions in **Table 3.1** are observed and/or forecast to occur within 1 hour. Weather personnel are required to log on to an ADS and be prepared to supplement whenever a watch or warning has been issued for tornadic activity. Weather technicians are not required to supplement during airfield closure hours for other **Table 3.1** criteria. **Note**: This does not relieve EUs of their AFI 10-229, *Responding to Severe Weather Events*, AFI 15-128, *Air Force Weather Roles and Responsibilities* and AFMAN 15-129, Volume 2, *Air Force Weather Operations – Exploitation*, responsibilities for responding to severe weather events during non-duty hours. EUs will continue to have SWAP in place to respond to severe weather threats. EUs should concentrate their SWAP efforts on eyes forward resource protection and notification efforts during airfield closure hours.

Table 3.1. Summary of Mandatory

Mandatory Supplementary Weather Conditions - Body of Report (Note 1.)
Tornado (**+FC**) (Note 2) (Note 3)
Funnel Cloud (**FC**) (Note 2) (Note 3)
Waterspout (**+FC**) (Note 2) (Note 3)
Hail (**GR**) (local warning criteria only)
Volcanic Ash (**VA**)
Sandstorms (**SS**) or Duststorms (**DS**) (Note 4) (If local warning required)
Ice Pellets (IP)
Visibility <1/4 mile (400 meters) (AN/FMQ-19 only -- if locally required)
Mandatory Supplementary Weather Conditions- Remarks Section of Report (Note 1.)
Funnel Cloud **(Tornadic Activity _B/ E(hh)mm_LOC/DIR_(MOV))** (Note 2)   Snow Depth (Note 4) (only during airfield operating hours and if heavy snow warning has been issued and snowfall is occurring)
NOTES: 1. References for coding of augmentable weather conditions are located in Chapter 13.   2. The immediate reporting of funnel clouds takes precedence over any other phenomena.   3. Log on to AMOS and be prepared to supplement for tornadic activity anytime a weather watch or warning has been issued for the phenomena.   4. All Remarks and Additive Data references are provided in **Attachment 3**.

3.3.1. Supplementing remarks. Remarks will be added when supplementing for the above criteria. **Note:** When operating in an auto mode, the FMQ-19 generates the full range of required <u>automated</u> remarks listed in **Attachment 3**. In contrast, the FMQ-22 and TMQ-53 are only capable of generating the lightning and sea level pressure automated remarks. Weather organizations using the FMQ-22 or TMQ-53 are not required to manually supplement an observation with the additional automated remarks found in **Attachment 3**. Future ADS software patches will be fielded to correct this issue. Weather organizations using the FMQ-22 and TMQ-53 are still required to supplement and back-up for all other required non-automated remarks listed in **Attachment 3**.

3.3.2. Supplementing Tornadic Activity. Tornado(s), waterspout(s), or funnel cloud(s) will be reported in a METAR/SPECI IAW **Attachment 2** whenever they are observed to begin (first seen), are in progress, or disappear (end).

3.3.3. Supplementing Hail. Hail will be reported in a METAR/SPECI when hail meeting local warning criteria begins, is in progress or ends. Depth of hail on the ground is not reported in the METAR/SPECI report. When hail is supplemented in the body of the report, a remark should be included to report the beginning or ending time, unless the SPECI time is the beginning or ending time of the hail. When required to supplement, the weather technician should report the hailstone size in remarks. Refer to **Attachment 3**, for reporting hailstone size.

3.3.4. Supplementing Volcanic Ash. Volcanic Ash will be reported whenever it is observed. Refer to **Chapter 8** and **Attachment 3**, for reporting volcanic ash.

3.3.5. **Supplementing Sand Storms/Dust Storms.** Sandstorms/Duststorms will be reported whenever a local warning for the condition is required.

3.4. Back-up of an AMOS. Except for some automated remarks, back-up refers to weather technicians providing the same reporting capability as that provided by the AMOS. Weather technicians will back-up the AMOS equipment if the system/sensor(s) is/are not operational or unavailable due to sensor and/or communication failure. Weather technicians will make every attempt to immediately log out any broken equipment, except when immediate flight safety (e.g., in-flight emergency) warrants otherwise. Weather technicians are not required to immediately log a system/sensor out if a deficiency report is currently published by AFWA. Weather technicians do not need to log out the AMOS as the result of a system restart. Refer to AFI 21-103, *Equipment Inventory, Status and Utilization Reporting*, for additional information. EU leadership will use sound ORM practices to develop/document those operationally significant weather thresholds (normally provided by a fully operational AMOS) to report while operating in back-up mode. There is no requirement to back-up the system/sensor when the airfield is closed. Weather technicians will provide back-up information IAW **Attachment 2** and **Attachment 3**. Back-up information is required for longline dissemination, for OWS terminal aerodrome forecast (TAF) production and for local ground-to-air dissemination to sustain air operations at the airfield (e.g., ATC functions and/or the Automatic Terminal Information Service (ATIS)). Use manual observing procedures for individual elements when performing back-up operations. Weather technicians will not replace the entire automated observation with a manual observation when backing-up malfunctioning sensors.

3.5. Back-up Equipment. EUs should use available equipment (e.g., AN/FMQ-19 discontinuity sensors, AN/TMQ-53, hand-held weather device (e.g., Kestrel®), or other MAJCOM or AFWA-approved equipment to back-up AMOSs).

3.5.1. Conditions for using an AN/TMQ-53 in a back-up mode. EUs may use the AN/TMQ-53 as a primary or back-up without estimating values if all the following conditions are met:

3.5.1.1. The AN/TMQ-53 equipment is in good working condition (e.g., operating properly) and properly maintained IAW the TO and established maintenance schedules.

3.5.1.2. The equipment is set up and operated IAW the T.O. and is sited IAW FCM-S4-1994, Chapters 3 and 4. **Note:** The TMQ-53 has known sensor height exposure limitations. However, if the siting requirement in Chapters 3 and 4 are met, the values obtained are not estimated.

3.5.1.3. The values from the AN/TMQ-53 equipment are representative and consistent with the values from surrounding observing sites (if available).

3.5.2. Wind and pressure values from any piece of back-up equipment (e.g., hand-held devices or other deployable meteorological equipment), other than a properly sited and maintained AN/TMQ-53, will be estimated.

3.5.3. Unrepresentative Values. Unrepresentative meteorological values from any equipment will not be included in the observation. These values will be considered missing (**M**) if the value cannot be determined by other means.

3.6. Maintenance Procedures. Maintenance procedures for each system are outlined in the applicable system TO. In addition to the TO procedures, weather technicians will ensure supported ATC agencies are notified of all outages prior to contacting any maintenance agency. Notify the AFWA Fielded Systems Service Center (FSSC) when airfield systems personnel are repairing/replacing parts on any AMOS equipped with a remote maintenance capability (e.g., an AN/FMQ-19). The AFWA FSSC should not be notified of ASOS outages; use local procedures instead.

Chapter 4

OBSERVATION FORM ENTRIES

4.1. Introduction. This chapter contains instructions for making entries on Form 3813 provided by the ADS and AF 3803.

4.2. ADS Procedures. EUs with an ADS (e.g., JET) will use the Form 3813 to encode/disseminate all METAR and SPECI observation data.

4.2.1. The Form 3813 is an electronically generated official record of daily surface weather observations and summary data.

4.2.2. The ADS has the ability to store data on the Form 3813 and electronically transmit it to the 14WS for processing and archive; however, EUs may manually edit and send the form to the 14WS at an appropriate time, usually at the beginning of the next duty day (not to exceed 7 days).

4.2.3. Only position qualified weather technicians are authorized to make entries on the Form 3813 during augmentation. Trainees may make form entries only when under the immediate supervision of a position-qualified weather technician who attests to the validity of the entries.

4.2.4. The Form 3813 automatically populates some of the Summary of Day (SOD) data fields as the observations are entered on the ADS. The weather technician will enter or correct data as needed.

4.2.5. The National Climatic Data Center and 14WS automatically collect weather observations and summary of the day information from automated ASOS-equipped locations that use the Advanced Weather Interactive Processing System (AWIPS) to disseminate their observations.

4.2.6. Single element LOCALs for altimeter setting can be entered in the ADS Form 3813 for dissemination. If passed by voice, altimeter LOCALs can be recorded on AF 3803 if not recorded on a local dissemination log or a tape recording. If altimeter LOCALs are input into an ADS (e.g., JET), the temperature and dew point must also be encoded for the ADS to properly calculate PA and DA.

4.3. Non-ADS Procedures. EUs not equipped with ADS will use an electronic or paper AF 3803 or the approved electronic workbook version (Excel®) of Form 3803 (available: **https://notus2.afccc.af.mil/SCIS/form3803info.asp**.). Paper or electronic forms are an official record of daily surface weather observations and summary data.

4.3.1. The form may be printed out as a paper version at non-ADS EUs. Start a new form with the first observation of each new calendar day local standard time (LST).

4.3.2. EUs taking surface observations for deployed weather operations (classified or unclassified) will prepare the electronic or paper, AF 3803 in one copy. If using a paper copy of the AF 3803, data may be recorded for more than 1 day on the same sheet by entering the day and month of the next day's observations on a separate line following the last observation of the preceding day. If using the electronic version of the AF 3803, use a separate worksheet for each calendar day.

4.3.3. Only position-qualified weather technicians are authorized to make form entries. Trainees may make form entries only when under the immediate supervision of a position-qualified weather technician who attests to the validity of the entries by initialing in column 18 (trainee's initials go in Column 90 Remarks).

4.3.4. When paper AF 3803 is used, ensure legible copies and ample contrast (for photographic requirements) by using only a pencil with black grade 2 medium lead or a mechanical pencil (.5 mm or .7 mm) using only black HB or MH lead. AF 3803 hand-written entries will be all capital, block letters, or block numerals.

4.3.5. All METAR and SPECI observations will be recorded on the AF 3803. LOCAL altimeter setting observations do not need to be recorded on the form if a record of the observations is maintained on a local dissemination log, or a tape-recording. When in doubt, record the LOCAL.

4.3.6. Separation of Data. Use a blank space in column 13 to separate data. Do not use a solidus (/).

4.3.7. Missing Data. When an element does not occur or cannot be observed, the corresponding group and preceding space are omitted from that particular report. Briefly explain in column 90 (Remarks, Notes, and Miscellaneous Phenomena) the reasons for missing data. This does not apply to elements that can be obtained by estimation or alternate methods of determination (e.g., sky condition, visibility, present weather, wind, pressure).

4.3.8. Late Observations. When a METAR is taken late, but within 15 minutes of the standard time of observation, and no appreciable changes (SPECI criteria) have occurred since the standard time, enter the observation in black and transmit as a METAR using the standard time of observation. If conditions have changed appreciably or the observation is more than 15 minutes late, skip a line, then record and transmit a SPECI. After transmitting the SPECI, return to the skipped line and, using the standard time of the missed observation, record an observation in RED using estimates of the conditions probable at the time of the missed observation, using data from recording instruments whenever possible. Enter "FIBI" (Contraction for *Filed But Impractical to Transmit*) in parentheses in Column 13. This observation will not be transmitted.

4.3.9. Entering AF 3803 Synoptic Data and SOD data. The electronic AF 3803 has internal macros to calculate and populate the SOD data fields on the form. However, each of the SOD fields can also be edited by the weather technician, except for columns 68 and 69.

4.3.9.1. Time UTC (Column 41). On the line captioned MID TO (at units taking midnight LST observations), enter the beginning time of the first 6-hourly scheduled after 0000 LST. On the following four lines (captioned 1, 2, 3 and 4 in column 43), enter the beginning time of each 6-hourly observation. A time entry is not applicable to the MID line. Make all time entries in four figures to the nearest minute UTC. See **Figure 4.1**

Figure 4.1. Example AF 3803 Synoptic and Summary of the Day Entries

SURFACE WEATHER OBSERVATIONS (METAR/SPECI)						LATITUDE 30° 10'N	LONGITUDE 79° 01'W	STATION ELEVATION +218 Feet (MSL)	
SYNOPTIC DATA						SUMMARY OF DAY			
TIME (UTC) (41)	TIME (LST) (42)	NO (43)	PRECIP (water equiv.) (44)	SNOW FALL (45)	SNOW DEPTH (46)	24-HR MAX TEMP (°C) (66)	PRECIP (water equiv.) (68)	SNOW FALL (69)	SNOW DEPTH (70)
MID (LST) TO: 0550	MID TO: 0050		0.02	0.0		28	0.91	•T	0
0550	0050	(1)	0.05	0.0	0				
1150	0650	(2)	0.00	0.0	0	24-HR MIN TEMP (°C) (67)	SPEED (knots) (71)	DRCTN (true) (72)	TIME (UTC) (73)
1750	1250	(3)	0.00	0.0	0				
2350	1850	(4)	0.89	•T	0	06	53	260	1854
MID (LST)	MID (LST)		T	0.0	0				

4.3.9.2. Time LST (Column 42). Enter the LST equivalent to the time UTC entered in column 41.

4.3.9.3. Observation Number (Column 43). No entry required. This column provides a reference to the lines used for the midnight and 6-hourly observations. Entries in columns 41 through 45 are made on the first line of this column to record precipitation amounts for the period from midnight LST to the first 6-hourly observation of the day. Entries in columns 41 through 46 are made on the lines captioned 1, 2, 3 and 4 to record 6-hourly precipitation amounts and snow depth data at the respective synoptic observation times of the day. Entries in columns 44 through 46 are made on the last line to record precipitation amounts for the period from the last 6-hourly observation to midnight LST. No entries are made on the lines captioned MID TO and MID in time zones where midnight LST corresponds to the time of a 6-hourly observation.

4.3.9.4. Precipitation (Column 44). On the MID TO line (at units taking midnight LST observations), enter the amount of precipitation (water equivalent) that has occurred between the midnight LST observation and the first 6-hourly observation time. At 6-hourly observation times, on the applicable lines 1, 2, 3 and 4, enter the amount of precipitation occurring in the 6 hours before the respective 6-hourly observation. On the MID line (at units taking midnight LST observations), enter the amount of precipitation that has occurred between the last 6-hourly observation and the midnight LST observation. Enter 0 if no precipitation occurred in the period; enter a T for a trace (amounts of less than 0.005-inch). If no precipitation has occurred before actual precipitation observation time, but is observed to occur before coding of the observation, enter T even though a measurable amount may have occurred. Enter measurable amounts to the nearest 0.01inch.

4.3.9.4.1. Water Equivalent. Whenever the water equivalent of frozen precipitation cannot be measured (e.g., by melting a core sampling), enter the estimated water equivalent on the basis of a 1:10 ratio, or other ratio where there is evidence that a different ratio is more appropriate for the individual storm or location. Prefix estimated values (except 0 or T) with the symbol E, and enter a remark in column 90 to indicate the ratio used (e.g., E - 1:15 RATIO USED).

4.3.9.4.2. Limited-Duty Units. Use the following procedures for the first precipitation observations at limited-duty units (those operating less than 24 hours per day) where one or more 6-hourly observations are not made.

4.3.9.4.2.1. Determine and enter the total accumulation of precipitation since the last recorded 6-hourly observation. Except as specified below, make this entry at the time of the current 6-hourly observation.

4.3.9.4.2.2. At units opening between 1200 and 1400 UTC, determine this precipitation data at the time of the first METAR of the day and enter it on the line corresponding to the 1200Z 6-hourly observation.

4.3.9.4.2.3. Prefix the entry (other than 0) with an asterisk, and enter a remark in column 90 to indicate the actual time period applicable to the amount (e.g., *.11 in column 44 and *12-HR PCPN in column 90). At units that do not operate on weekends or holidays, the column 90 remark might be *72-HR PCPN.

4.3.9.5. Snowfall (Column 45). On the MID TO line (at units taking midnight observations), enter the amount of solid precipitation that has occurred between the midnight observation and the first 6-hourly observation time. At 6-hourly observation times, on the applicable lines 1, 2, 3 and 4, enter the amount of the frozen precipitation occurring in the 6 hours before the respective 6-hourly observations. On the MID lines (at units taking midnight LST observations), enter the amount of precipitation that has occurred between the last 6-hourly observation and the midnight LST observation.

4.3.9.5.1. Frozen Precipitation. Enter 0 if no frozen precipitation fell in the period. Enter T for a trace (less than 0.05 inch), and if precipitation melted as it fell, enter a remark in column 90 (e.g., T--MELTED AS IT FELL). If no frozen precipitation has occurred before actual precipitation observation time but is observed to occur before coding of the observation, enter T even though a measurable amount may have occurred.

4.3.9.5.1.1. For a measurable amount, enter the maximum depth of frozen precipitation accumulated in the period to the nearest 0.1-inch. If several occurrences of frozen precipitation occurred in the period (e.g., snow showers) and each fall melted either completely or in part before the next fall occurred, enter the total of the maximum depths accumulated by each of the falls.

4.3.9.5.1.2. Prefix estimated amounts (except 0 or T) with an E, and enter an appropriate remark in column 90 (e.g., E--ESTIMATED DUE TO MELTING).

4.3.9.5.1.3. Enter an asterisk as a prefix to the amount if it consists entirely of hail; enter *HAIL in column 90.

4.3.9.5.2. Limited-Duty Unit Procedures. Use the following procedures for the first precipitation observation at limited-duty units where one or more 6-hourly observations are not made.

4.3.9.5.2.1. Determine and enter the total accumulation of frozen precipitation since the last recorded 6-hourly observation.

4.3.9.5.2.2. At units opening between 1200 and 1400 UTC, determine this precipitation data at the time of the first METAR of the day and enter it on the line corresponding to the 1200Z 6-hourly observation.

4.3.9.5.2.3. Prefix the entry (other than 0) with an asterisk and enter a remark in column 90 to indicate the actual time period applicable to the amount (e.g., *.1 in column 45 and *12-HR PCPN in column 90). At units that do not operate on weekends, the column 90 remark might be *72-HR PCPN.

4.3.9.6. Snow Depth (Column 46). Enter the depth of frozen precipitation and ice on the ground at the time of each 6-hourly observation on the lines captioned 1, 2, 3 and 4 and at the time of the midnight LST observation, if applicable, on the line captioned MID. Enter 0 if there is no frozen precipitation or ice on the ground in exposed areas (snow may be present in forested or otherwise protected areas). Enter T for a trace (less than 0.5-inch) on the ground in representative areas. If no solid precipitation or ice is on the ground at the actual precipitation observation time but is observed to occur before coding of the observation, enter T even though a measurable amount may have occurred. Enter measurable depths to the nearest whole inch.

4.3.9.6.1. Melted Snow Reporting Procedure. If snow melted during the period, prefix the current depth with an asterisk. Enter the maximum depth and the approximate time UTC of occurrence in column 90 (e.g., MAX SNOW DEPTH 1 AT 1530).

4.3.9.6.2. Hail Reporting Procedure. Prefix the depth with an asterisk if it consists entirely of hail and enter *HAIL in column 90.

4.3.9.6.3. Limited-Duty Unit Procedures. Use the following procedures for the first precipitation observation at limited-duty units where one or more 6-hourly observations are not made.

4.3.9.6.3.1. Determine and enter the total depth of frozen precipitation on the ground at the time of the first 6-hourly observation.

4.3.9.6.3.2. At units opening between 1200 and 1400 UTC, determine this data at the time of the first METAR of the day and enter it on the line corresponding to the 1200Z 6-hourly observation. This depth is also entered in column 70 and requires a remark to indicate the time applicable to the amount.

4.3.9.7. 24-Hour Precipitation (Column 68). Enter the total precipitation (water equivalent) for the 24 hours ending at midnight LST. The entry is normally based on a summation of entries in column 44. However, where midnight LST observations are taken, do not include the value of the first 6-hourly observation entered in column 44 when adding column 44 amounts to determine the column 68 entry. Enter 0 if no precipitation occurred in the period. Enter T for a trace (less than 0.005 inch). The sum of all trace entries (from column 44) is a trace unless the unit is equipped with a recording or totaling gauge that indicates 0.005-inch or more. Prefix amounts (except 0 or T) with an E when the total includes an estimated amount. At limited-duty units that do not take a midnight LST observation, make this entry using a summation of the column 44 entries even though the amounts are not limited to the LST day. Prefix amounts (except 0 or T) with an E.

4.3.9.8. 24-Hour Snowfall (Column 69). Enter the total amount of frozen precipitation that has fallen in the 24 hours ending at midnight LST. The entry is normally based on a summation of entries in column 45. Where midnight LST observations are taken, do not include the value of the first 6-hourly observation entered in column 45. Enter 0 if no frozen precipitation fell during the period. Enter T for a trace (less than 0.05-inch); if the frozen precipitation melted as it fell, enter T--MELTED AS IT FELL in column 90. The sum of all trace entries is a trace unless the unit is equipped with a recording or totaling gauge that indicates 0.05-inch or more. For a measurable amount, enter the total amount that has fallen to the nearest 0.1-inch. The amount entered must be that which has accumulated in the past 24 hours adjusted for any melting or evaporation having taken place. Prefix the amount with an asterisk if it consists entirely of hail and enter *HAIL in column 90. Prefix an estimated amount with an E, and enter a remark in column 90 (e.g., E—ESTIMATED DUE TO MELTING). At limited-duty units not taking a midnight LST observation, make this entry using a summation of the column 45 entries even though the amounts are not limited to the LST day. Prefix amounts (except 0 or T) with an E.

4.3.9.9. Snow Depth (Column 70). Enter the depth of frozen precipitation and ice on the ground at 1200 UTC or as directed by MAJCOM or higher headquarters. The entry is basically the same as that in column 46 for the 1200Z observation. If personnel are not on duty at 1200 UTC, enter depth as measured as near to 1200 UTC as practical, and for a non-zero entry in Column 70, enter a remark in column 90 to indicate the time UTC (e.g., COL 70 ENTRY OBSVD AT 1120). Enter 0 if there is no frozen precipitation or ice on the ground in exposed areas (snow may be present in surrounding forested or otherwise protected areas). Enter T for a trace (less than 0.5 inch) on the ground in representative areas. Enter a measurable depth on the ground at the time of observation to the nearest whole inch. Prefix the amount with an asterisk if it consists entirely of hail and enter *HAIL in column 90.

4.4. Corrections. Disseminate a correction immediately after detecting an error in a transmitted report. Do not send a correction long-line if superseded by a later report. All hand written entries must be legible.

4.4.1. Correct errors discovered before dissemination (all columns, electronic or paper forms) by deleting or erasing, as applicable, the erroneous data from the form and entering the correct data in black (font or pencil). Erasing entries on the paper form is authorized only if the data has not been disseminated (either locally or long-line).

4.4.2. Correct errors discovered after either local or long-line dissemination as follows:

4.4.2.1. Form 3813. If an error is discovered after dissemination, but before another observation has been disseminated, select the observation type (SA-C, SP-C, or L-C) as applicable. Enter the original time of the observation to be corrected and re-enter the entire observation with the corrected data. Enter "COR (time)" in remarks (Column 13) representing the time the correction is being disseminated (refer to **Attachment 3**). Select the "Submit Observation" button to disseminate the corrected observation locally and long-line. The letters "COR" will appear in the new observation after the unit's ICAO. If an error is discovered after dissemination and after another observation has been disseminated, follow the same procedures above, except do not enter "COR (time)" in remarks and select the "Save to Form Only" button after entering the corrected observation. The observation will not be disseminated locally or long-line, but will be saved to the Form 3813.

4.4.2.2. AF 3803 Electronic or Paper. Make corrections according to the following procedures. All corrected data and Column 13 & 90 remarks will be in **RED FONT**.

4.4.2.2.1. Columns 1 through 13.

4.4.2.2.1.1. Electronic 3803. Enter the correct data in the appropriate field. In column 13, annotate "COR FROM," followed by the appropriate identification, the **ORIGINAL ENTRY**, and the time of the correction. For example, if the original (incorrect) temperature entry was 20, and it was corrected to 21 at 1430, the column 13 remark would read COR FROM TEMP 20 @ 1430 (in red), and the temperature block would be 21 (in red). For corrections not transmitted locally or long-line, no time reference is required.

4.4.2.2.1.2. Paper 3803. Make corrected entries in red pencil on the original. Enter corrections by drawing a line through the erroneous data and entering the correct data above it or on the next lower line. If space is insufficient, enter the correction in column 13 with an appropriate identification (e.g., TEMP 25). If the correction is disseminated locally, or locally and long-line, enter COR in column 13 followed by the time (to the nearest minute UTC) the correction was locally disseminated. In the case of long-line-only dissemination (e.g., a correction for additive data), enter COR and the approximate UTC time the correction was transmitted.

4.4.2.2.2. Columns 15 through 90.

4.4.2.2.2.1. Electronic 3803. Enter the correct data in the appropriate field, and then annotate the corrections. For errors in columns 15 through 21, annotate "COR FROM" in **column 13** followed by the appropriate identification, the **ORIGINAL ENTRY**, and the time of the correction. For example, if the original (incorrect) station pressure entry was 29.370, and it was corrected to 29.375 at 1530, the column 13 remark would read COR FROM STA PRES 29.370 @ 1530, and the station pressure block would be 29.375. For errors in columns 22 through 90, annotate "COR FROM" in **column 90**, followed by the appropriate identification, the **ORIGINAL ENTRY**, and the time of the correction. For example, if the original (incorrect) snow depth entry was 40, and it was corrected to 42 at 1430, the column **90** remark would read COR FROM SNOW DEPTH 40 @ 1430, and the snow depth block would be 42. For corrections not transmitted locally or long-line, no time reference is required.

4.4.2.2.2.2. Paper 3803. For an error resulting in erroneous data being disseminated locally or long-line, draw a **BLACK** line through the erroneous entry, and enter the correct data **IN BLACK** on the next line beneath it. If space is insufficient, enter the correction in column 90 with an appropriate identification (e.g., 1758 STA PRES 29.375).

4.4.2.2.3. For other corrections delete or erase the erroneous entry and enter the correct data.

4.5. Transfer and Disposition of Observation Records. ADS-equipped EUs, except ASOS locations with AWIPS, will conduct quality assurance on the electronic Form 3813 and send the form to the 14WS, usually at the beginning of the next duty day (not to exceed 7 days). E-mail Form 3813s to "observation_3813@afccc.af.mil." EUs without an ADS should complete the approved electronic worksheet version (Excel®) of Form 3803 (available: https://notus2.afccc.af.mil/SCIS/form3803info.asp.) at the beginning of each month. E-mail the previous month's zipped workbook as an attachment to 14WS at observation_3803@afccc.af.mil. **Note**: E-mail addresses may change. EUs without the capability to email the electronic 3803 forms (workbooks) will send either a CD containing the workbook or the original hard-copy forms to:

14 WS/WXD
151 Patton Avenue, Room 120
Asheville, NC 28801-5002

4.5.1. Weather technicians operating in deployed environments will coordinate with 14WS for timely transmission and receipt of their forms. At a minimum, every effort will be documented to reflect coordination (pre-operation, during or post) with the 14 WS to outline data collection efforts.

4.5.2. Once official observation records are transmitted to 14WS for processing and archiving, maintain electronic or paper copies for 30-days. The USAF RDS on the AFRIMS webpage is the guidance for records management and disposition.

4.5.3. EUs will ensure all paper forms sent to 14WS have no cuts, tears, stains, or staples. 14WS digitizes the forms for permanent record.

Chapter 5

WIND

5.1. Introduction. This chapter prescribes the observing and reporting standards for wind data in automated and augmented reports. Wind is measured in terms of velocity, a vector that includes direction and speed. The direction and speed of the wind should be measured in an unobstructed area. This will avoid, to a large degree, measuring wind directions and speeds that have been disturbed by local obstructions and will result in a report more representative of the general weather patterns.

5.2. Definitions.

5.2.1. Wind. For surface observation purposes, wind is the horizontal motion of the air past a given point.

5.2.2. Wind Direction. The direction from which the wind is blowing.

5.2.3. Variable Wind Direction. Variable wind direction may be reported when the average wind speed is 6 knots or less in the preceding 2 minutes or when the wind direction varies by 60 degrees or more with an average wind speed greater than 6 knots in the preceding 2 minutes.

5.2.4. Wind Shift. A term applied to a change in wind direction by 45 degrees or more in less than 15 minutes with sustained winds of 10 knots or more throughout the wind shift.

5.2.5. Wind Speed. The rate of movement of air past a given point. Refer to Table 5.4 to convert miles per hour to knots and Table 5.5 to convert knots to miles per hour.

5.2.6. Calm Wind. The term used to describe the absence of any apparent motion of the air.

5.2.7. Gust. Maximum wind speed observed during the 10-minute observation period indicated by rapid fluctuations in wind speed with a variation of 10 knots or more between peaks and lulls.

5.2.8. Peak Wind Speed. The highest (maximum) wind speed observed or recorded.

5.3. Wind Algorithms for AMOSs. The AMOS wind algorithm uses 5-second average wind directions and speeds to compute 2-minute averages for reporting direction and speed. The 5-second average speed represents an instantaneous wind and is used to determine gusts, squalls and peak wind data. The 2-minute average direction is used to determine wind shifts and the range of variability for variable wind direction reports. The wind direction and speed sensors provide the system processor with sufficient data to compute 5-second and 2-minute average wind speeds and directions.

5.4. Determining Standards. Table 5.1 may be used for quick reference of wind elements, but the instructions below should be read to fully understand the wind determining standards. Report and encode wind conditions IAW Chapter 13. AMOS sensors determine the wind direction, speed, character, wind shifts and peak wind at all automated observing locations.

5.4.1. Wind Direction. Direction is measured in tens of degrees with reference to true north. The wind direction is determined by averaging the direction over a 2-minute period. **Note:** OCONUS EUs at locations where the host nation is responsible for the airfield observation will ensure DoD aircrews are aware of how winds are measured/reported by the local ATC agency (e.g., 2-minute or 10-minute averaged winds).

5.4.2. Variable Wind Direction. If the range of variability in wind direction observed during the 2-minute period meets the definition specified in paragraph 5.2., the wind direction is considered variable and will be reported IAW Chapter 13.

5.4.3. Wind Speed. Wind speed is measured in whole knots. The wind speed is determined by averaging the speed over a 2-minute period.

5.4.4. Wind Character. The wind speed data for the most recent 10 minutes is examined to evaluate the occurrence of gusts.

5.4.5. Peak Wind Speed. Peak wind data is determined by using the internal storage of wind data. The peak wind speed is the highest instantaneous wind speed measured since the last METAR observation. The peak wind data is reported in the remarks of a METAR whenever the peak wind speed exceeds 25 knots. The format for the remark is in Attachment 3.

5.4.6. Wind Shifts. If conditions meeting the definition of a wind shift specified in paragraph 5.2. are met, a wind shift has occurred and will be reported IAW Chapter 13. Wind shifts are often associated with the following phenomena:

5.4.6.1. Frontal passage. Winds shift in a clockwise manner in the Northern Hemisphere. Winds shift in a counterclockwise manner in the Southern Hemisphere.

5.4.6.2. Rapid drop or rise in temperature and/or dew point.

5.4.6.3. Rapid rise or drop in pressure.

5.4.6.4. Thunderstorm activity with lightning and hail, rainshowers or snowshowers.

Table 5.1. Summary of Wind Observing Standards.

Data	Wind Observing Standards
Wind Direction	2-minute average in 10-degree increments with respect to true north.
Wind Speed	2-minute average in knots.
Wind Gust	The maximum instantaneous speed in knots in the past 10 minutes.
Peak Wind	The maximum instantaneous speed in knots (since the last METAR) reported whenever the peak is greater than 25 knots.
Wind Shift	A change in wind direction by 45 degrees or more in less than 15 minutes with sustained winds of 10 knots or greater throughout the shift.

5.5. Manual Observing Methods.

5.5.1. Determine wind direction, speed, character, wind shifts and peak wind at the touchdown area of the active runway. During an outage of the primary (in-use) sensor, determine data using other reliable sources. Data obtained from alternate equipment may be used as a guide for determining winds when the primary sensor output is considered unrepresentative.

5.5.2. Wind Direction.

5.5.2.1. Values from digital wind instruments are in reference to magnetic North and may be reported locally. These values must be converted to true for observational records and longline dissemination. Locations in extreme northern latitudes, such as Thule AB, Greenland, may report true wind direction locally when runway heading have been changed to reflect true.

5.5.2.2. Where instruments are inoperative or not available, determine the magnetic wind direction by using a compass and observing the wind cone, tree movement of twigs or leaves, smoke, etc., or by facing into the wind in an unsheltered area. When determining wind direction, note that even small obstacles may cause variations in the wind direction. Do not use the movement of clouds, regardless of how low they are, in determining the surface wind direction. Convert the wind direction from magnetic to true before transmitting longline. Add WND DATA ESTMD column remark in column 13.

5.5.3. Wind Speed. If an instrument value is not available, use the Beaufort scale (see **Table 5.2**) as a guide in determining the wind speed. Add WND DATA ESTMD remark in column 13.

Table 5.2. Beaufort Scale of Winds

Wind Equivalent -- Beaufort Scale				
Beaufort #	MPH	KTS	International Description	Specifications
0	<1	<1	Calm	Calm; smoke rises vertically.
1	1-3	1-3	Light Air	Direction of wind shown by smoke drift not by wind vanes.
2	4-7	4-6	Light Breeze	Wind felt on face; leaves rustle; vanes moved by wind.
3	8-12	7-10	Gentle Breeze	Leaves and small twigs in constant motion; wind extends light flag.
4	13-18	11-16	Moderate Breeze	Raises dust, loose paper; small branches moved.
5	19-24	17-21	Fresh Breeze	Small trees in leaf begin to sway; crested wavelets form on inland waters.
6	25-31	22-27	Strong Breeze	Large branches in motion; whistling heard in overhead wires; umbrellas used with difficulty.
7	32-38	28-33	Near Gale	Whole trees in motion; inconvenience felt walking against the wind.
8	39-46	34-40	Gale	Breaks twigs off trees; impedes progress.
9	47-54	41-47	Strong Gale	Slight structural damage occurs.
10	55-63	48-55	Storm	Trees uprooted; considerable damage occurs.
11	64-72	56-63	Violent Storm	Widespread damage.
12	73-82	64-71	Hurricane	

5.5.4. Peak Wind Data. If the wind record is incomplete, data from it may still be used provided there is no indication that the peak wind speed occurred during the period of the missing data. If you believe the peak wind data occurred during a time that no wind record was available, consider the data missing.

5.5.4.1. If the wind direction record is incomplete, estimate the direction (e.g., from past directions or from surrounding stations, if representative) to the nearest 10 degrees for remarks on peak wind speed and for peak wind of the day. If the outage period is so extensive a peak gust direction cannot be reasonably estimated, or if no wind record is available, consider the data missing.

5.5.4.2. EUs with multiple sensor locations use the last highest speed observed for the appropriate period, regardless of the active runway at the time of occurrence.

Table 5.3. Conversion of Miles Per Hour to Knots

Conversion of Miles Per Hour to Knots									
M P H	0	1	2	3	4	5	6	7	8	9
	KTS	KTS	KTS	KTS	KTS	KTS	KTS	KTS	KTS	KTS
0	0	1	2	3	3	4	5	6	7	8
10	9	10	10	11	12	13	14	15	16	17
20	17	18	19	20	21	22	23	23	24	25
30	26	27	28	29	30	30	31	32	33	34
40	35	36	36	37	38	39	40	41	42	43
50	43	44	45	46	47	48	49	50	50	51
60	52	53	54	55	56	56	57	58	59	60
70	61	62	63	63	64	65	66	67	68	69
80	70	70	71	72	73	74	75	76	76	77
90	78	79	80	81	82	83	83	84	85	86
NOTE: This table is not reversible. Use Table 5.5. to convert knots to miles per hour.										

Table 5.4. Conversion of Knots to Miles Per Hour

Conversion of Knots to Miles Per Hour									
K T S	0	1	2	3	4	5	6	7	8	9
	MPH	MPH	MPH	MPH	MPH	MPH	MPH	MPH	MPH	MPH
0	0	1	2	3	5	6	7	8	9	10
10	12	13	14	15	16	17	18	20	21	22
20	23	24	25	26	28	29	30	31	32	33
30	35	36	37	38	39	40	41	43	44	45
40	46	47	48	49	51	52	53	54	55	56
50	58	59	60	61	62	63	64	66	67	68
60	69	70	71	72	74	75	76	77	78	79
70	81	82	83	84	85	86	87	89	90	91
80	92	93	94	96	97	98	99	100	101	102
90	104	105	106	107	108	109	110	112	113	114
NOTE: This table is not reversible. Use Table 5.4. to convert miles per hour to knots.										

Chapter 6

VISIBILITY

6.1. Introduction. This chapter prescribes the observing and reporting standards for visibility data in automated and augmented reports. Visibility is a measure of the opacity of the atmosphere and is expressed in terms of the horizontal distance at which a person is able to see and identify specified objects. Visibility values are generally reported in statute miles at U.S. locations (including Hawaii, Alaska and Guam) and the unit of measurement will be the same as that published for the installation in DoD FLIP airfield approach plate minimums.

6.2. Definitions. Note: The following definitions are for manual observation methods, to include augmented observations. AMOSs calculate visibility values differently. See **Chapter 13** for more information on automated visibility reporting.

6.2.1. Visibility. The greatest horizontal distance at which selected objects can be seen and identified.

6.2.2. Prevailing Visibility. The visibility considered to be representative of the visibility conditions at the official observing point. It is the greatest visibility equaled or exceeded throughout at least half the horizon circle, not necessarily continuous (e.g., it may be composed of sectors distributed anywhere around the horizon circle).

6.2.3. Variable Prevailing Visibility. A condition where the prevailing visibility is less than 3 statute miles (4800 meters) and is rapidly increasing and/or decreasing by 1/2 mile (0800 meters) or more during the period of observation.

6.2.4. Sector Visibility. The visibility in a specified direction that represents at least a 45-degree arc (portion) of the horizon circle.

6.2.5. Surface Visibility. The prevailing visibility determined from the designated point(s) of observation. It normally represents a value observed at a height of 6 feet (1.8 meters) above ground level.

6.2.6. Tower Visibility. The prevailing visibility determined from the control tower.

6.2.7. Visibility Markers. Dark or nearly dark objects viewed against the horizon sky during the day or unfocused lights of moderate intensity (about 25 candelas) during the night.

6.3. Visibility Algorithms for AMOS. The AMOS calculates average visibility using spatial time averaging of sensor data. Visibility is an evaluation of sensor data gathered during the 10-minute period ending at the actual time of the observation. The visibility data during the averaging period are examined to determine if variable visibility should be reported. Where the AMOS has meteorological discontinuity sensors, the data from the additional sensors are examined to determine if their values meet criteria for generating a visibility remark.

6.4. Determining Standards.

6.4.1. Reportable Visibility Values. The reportable visibility values in statute miles and meters are provided in **Table 6.1.** If the visibility falls halfway between two reportable values, the lower value will be reported.

6.4.2. Surface Visibility. Surface visibility is an evaluation of the prevailing visibility gathered during the 10-minute period ending at the actual time of the observation.

6.4.3. Variable Prevailing Visibility. When variable prevailing visibility conditions occur, meeting the definition in paragraph 6.2., variable visibility will be reported in the remarks IAW **Attachment 3.**

6.4.4. Visibility at Second Location. At observing locations equipped with two or more visibility sensors, the visibility at the designated discontinuity sensor will be encoded in remarks when the visibility at the second location is lower than the visibility in the body of the observation by a reportable value. The format for the remark is given in **Attachment 3.**

6.4.5. Visibility Sensor Range. Visibility sensors evaluate visibility from less than one-quarter statute mile (M1/4, M0400 meters) to 10 statute miles (9999 meters).

Table 6.1. Reportable Visibility Values

Automated Reportable Visibility Values		
M1/4 SM (M0400)	1 1/2 SM (2400)	5 SM (8000)
1/4 SM (0400)	1 3/4 SM (2800)	6 SM (9000)
1/2 SM (0800)	2 SM (3200)	7 SM (9999)
3/4 SM (1200)	2 1/2 SM (4000)	8 SM (9999)
1 SM (1600)	3 SM (4800)	9 SM (9999)
1 1/4 SM (2000)	4 SM (6000)	10 SM (9999)

6.5. Manual Observing Methods.

6.5.1. Visibility may be manually determined at the surface, the tower level or both. If visibility observations are made from just one level (e.g., the air traffic control tower), that level will be considered the "designated point of observation" and that visibility will be reported as surface visibility. If visibility observations are made from both levels, the visibility at the tower level may be reported as tower visibility.

6.5.2. Surface Visibility Observations. Determine and report surface visibility data as follows:

6.5.2.1. Point of Observation. The surface observation point should be as free from man-made obstructions as possible to view the entire horizon. Where obstructions exist, move to as many locations around the observation point as necessary and practicable within the period of observation to view as much of the horizon as possible. In this respect, natural obstructions, such as trees, hills, etc., are not obstructions to the horizon but define the horizon.

6.5.2.2. Prevailing Visibility. Evaluate visibility as frequently as practical. Using all available visibility markers, determine the greatest distances that can be seen in all directions around the horizon circle. Estimate the farthest distance that can be seen in each direction when the visibility is greater than the farthest marker(s). Base this estimate on the appearance of all visibility markers. If they are visible with sharp outlines and little blurring of color, the visibility is much greater than the distance to them. If a marker can barely be seen and identified, the visibility is about the same as the distance to the marker. The silhouette of mountains and hills against the sky and the brilliance of stars near the horizon may provide a useful guide to the general clarity of the atmosphere. Use the visibility values determined around the horizon circle as a basis for determining the prevailing visibility. Evaluate observed values using the following guidelines:

6.5.2.2.1. Under uniform conditions, consider the prevailing visibility to be the same as that determined in any direction around the horizon circle.

6.5.2.2.2. Under non-uniform conditions, use the values determined in the various sectors to determine the greatest distance seen throughout at least half the horizon circle (see example in Table 6.2).

Table 6.2. Example for Determining Prevailing Visibility

Visibility in Four Sectors			Visibility in Five Sectors		
SM	Meters	Approximate Degrees Encompassed	SM	Meters	Approximate Degrees Encompassed
5	8000	90	5	8000	100
2 1/2	4000	90	3	4800	90
2	3200	90	2 1/2	4000	60
1 1/2	2400	90	2	3200	50
			1 1/2	2400	60
Prevailing visibility is 2 1/2 (4000) because half of the horizon circle is at least 2 1/2 (4000).			Prevailing visibility is 3 (4800) because more than half of the horizon circle is at least 3 (4800).		

6.5.3. Variable Prevailing Visibility. If the prevailing visibility rapidly increases and/or decreases by 1/2 mile (0800 meters) or more during the time of the observation and the average prevailing visibility is less than 3 statute miles (4800 meters), the visibility is considered variable and the minimum and maximum visibility values observed will be reported in remarks. The format for the remark is given in Attachment 3.

6.5.4. Sector Visibility. When the visibility is not uniform in all directions, divide the horizon circle into arcs (sectors) that have uniform visibility and represent at least one eighth (1/8) of the horizon circle (45 degrees). The visibility that is evaluated in each sector is sector visibility. Sector visibility may be reported in remarks of weather observations when it differs from the prevailing visibility by one or more reportable value and either the prevailing or the sector visibility is less than 3 statute miles (4800 meters) or otherwise considered operationally significant. The format for the remark is given in Attachment 3.

Chapter 7

RUNWAY VISUAL RANGE

7.1. Introduction. This chapter contains information on Runway Visual Range (RVR) and the standards and procedures for the observing and determining of RVR, if locally required. All locations for which AF personnel record surface weather observations and have a requirement to report RVR, will report RVR according to the information stated on the airfield approach plates (e.g., statute miles/feet, meters/meters).

7.2. Definitions. The following are definitions used for determining runway visual range. Runway Visual Range is an instrumentally derived value that represents the horizontal distance that a pilot can see down the runway. The maximum distance in the direction of takeoff or landing at which the runway, or specified lights or markers delineating it, can be seen from a position above a specified point on its center line at a height corresponding to the average eye level of pilots at touch-down.

7.3. RVR Algorithms for AMOS. Most fixed-base AMOSs in the Air Force inventory will automatically sense and report RVR. **Note:** For OCONUS locations reporting RVR in meters, AMOSs determine RVR in 50-meter increments up to 800 meters, and in 100-meter increments up to 1500 meters, IAW WMO Manual on Codes (WMO-No. 306). This has a minor effect on the RVR special requirements (e.g., 0750 vs. 0730 meters), and may have an effect on flying units and the reporting of RVR minima listed in the FLIP for some overseas locations. EUs will coordinate RVR reporting in meters with ATC and other supported agencies. EUs will document local RVR reporting requirements in the base/host unit plans or a local weather support agreement.

7.4. Determining Standards. RVR will be determined when prevailing visibility is 1 statute mile (1600 meters) or less and/or RVR is 6000 feet (1500 meters) or less. The unit of measurement will be the same as that published for the installation in DoD FLIPs—generally feet in the CONUS and meters at OCONUS locations, unless otherwise determined locally. When no RVR minima are published in the DoD FLIPs, report locally in meters if prevailing visibility is locally disseminated in meters and in feet if prevailing visibility is reported locally in statute miles.

Table 7.1. RVR Reportable Values

AN/FMQ-19 CONUS (Feet)	AN/FMQ-19 OCONUS (Meters)	AN/FMQ-19 CONUS (Feet)	AN/FMQ-19 OCONUS (Meters)	AN/FMQ-19 CONUS (Feet)	AN/FMQ-19 OCONUS (Meters)
M0100			0400	3000	0900
0100	M0050	1400			1000
0200	0050		0450		1100
0300	0100	1600	0500	3500	
0400		1800	0550	4000	1200
0500	0150	2000	0600		1300
0600			0650	4500	
0700	0200	2200			1400
0800	0250		0700	5000	1500
0900		2400	0750	5500	P1500
1000	0300	2600	0800	6000	
1200	0350	2800		P6000	

7.5. Manual Observing Methods. Only RVR data obtained from a system providing a 10-minute RVR average readout will be disseminated longline. EUs without this capability will not manually measure RVR.

Chapter 8

PRESENT WEATHER

8.1. Introduction. This chapter describes the standards and procedures for automated and augmented observing, to include augmented observations, of present weather in METAR/SPECI reports. Present weather includes precipitation, obscurations (obstructions to visibility) and other weather phenomena, such as tornadic activity and sandstorms/dust storms. Present weather may be evaluated with instruments, manual methods or with a combination of the two.

8.2. Definitions. The following are simple definitions for types of precipitation, obscurations, and other weather phenomena. For more detailed definitions, refer to the Air Force Weather Specialty Qualification Training Package on *Observing*, or other references such as the American Meteorological Society *Glossary of Meteorology* or *Meteorology Today*. The acronym used in parenthesis following each type of precipitation, obscuration, or other weather phenomena denotes its standard notation in meteorological code. Reporting and encoding is covered in detail in Chapter 13.

8.2.1. Precipitation. Precipitation is any of the forms of water particles, whether in a liquid or solid state, that fall from the atmosphere and reach the ground. The various types are defined below:

8.2.1.1. Drizzle (DZ). DZ is a fairly uniform type of precipitation that is composed of fine drops with diameters of less than 0.02-inch (0.5 mm) that are very close together. DZ appears to float while following air currents. Unlike fog droplets, DZ does fall to the ground.

8.2.1.2. Rain (RA). RA comes in two forms. The first is in the form of drops larger than 0.02-inch (0.5 mm). The second can have smaller drops, but unlike DZ, they are widely separated.

8.2.1.3. Snow (SN). A solid form of precipitation which contains crystals, most of which are branched in the form of six-pointed stars.

8.2.1.4. Snow Grains (SG). Precipitation of very small, white, opaque grains of ice. When the grains hit hard ground, they do not bounce or shatter. They usually fall in small quantities, mostly from stratus type clouds and never as showers.

8.2.1.5. Ice Crystals (IC) (Diamond Dust). Precipitation that falls as unbranched ice crystals in the form of needles, columns or plates.

8.2.1.6. Ice Pellets (PL). PL are transparent or translucent pellets of ice, which are round or irregular, rarely conical and which have a diameter of 0.2 inch/5 mm or less. PL usually rebound when striking hard ground and makes a sound on impact. There are two main types. One type is composed of hard grains of ice consisting of frozen raindrops, or largely melted and refrozen snowflakes (formerly sleet). This type falls as continuous or intermittent precipitation. The second type consists of snow pellets encased in a thin layer of ice which has formed from the freezing, either of droplets intercepted by PL, or of water resulting from the partial melting of PL. This type falls as showers.

8.2.1.7. Hail (GR). Small balls or other pieces of ice falling separately or frozen together in irregular lumps exceeding 1/4 inch (5 mm) in diameter.

8.2.1.8. Small Hail and/or Snow Pellets (GS). GS are defined as white, opaque grains of ice. GS are round or sometimes conical with diameters less than 1/4 inch (5 mm). GS are brittle and easily crushed. When they fall on hard ground, they bounce and often break up.

8.2.1.9. Unknown Precipitation (UP). Precipitation that is reported when an AMOS precipitation discriminator detects, but cannot recognize, the type of precipitation.

8.2.2. Obscurations. Obscurations or obstructions to visibility can be any phenomenon in the atmosphere (not including precipitation) that reduces horizontal visibility to less than 7 statute miles (9999 meters). The various kinds are listed below:

8.2.2.1. Mist (BR) and Fog (FG). A visible aggregate of minute water particles suspended in the atmosphere. BR reduces visibility to less than 7 statute miles (9999 meters) but greater than or equal to 5/8 statute miles (1000 meters), while FG reduces visibility to less than 5/8 statute miles (1000 meters). It does not fall to the ground like DZ.

8.2.2.2. Smoke (FU). Small particles produced by combustion that are suspended in the air. A transition to haze may occur when smoke particles have traveled great distances (25 to 100 statute miles or more), and when the larger particles have settled out and the remaining particles have become widely scattered through the atmosphere.

8.2.2.3. Volcanic Ash (VA). Fine particles of rock powder that have erupted from a volcano and remain suspended in the atmosphere for long periods of time.

8.2.2.4. Widespread Dust (DU). Fine particles of earth or other matter raised or suspended in the air by the wind that may have occurred at or away from the unit.

8.2.2.5. Sand (SA). Particles of SA raised to a sufficient height that reduces visibility.

8.2.2.6. Haze (HZ). A suspension in the air of extremely small, dry particles invisible to the naked eye and sufficiently numerous to give it an opalescent appearance.

8.2.2.7. Spray (PY). An ensemble of water droplets torn by the wind from the surface of a large body of water, generally from the crest of waves, and carried a short distance into the air.

8.2.3. Other Weather Phenomena.

8.2.3.1. Well-Developed Dust/Sand Whirl (PO) (commonly referred to as Dust Devils). An ensemble of particles of dust or sand, sometimes accompanied by small pieces of litter, that is raised from the ground and takes the form of a whirling column with varying height, small diameter and an approximate vertical axis.

8.2.3.2. Squall (SQ). A strong wind characterized by a sudden onset in which the wind speed increases by at least 16 knots and is sustained at 22 knots or more for at least 1 minute.

8.2.3.3. Tornadic Activity.

8.2.3.3.1. Tornado. A violent, rotating column of air touching the ground. It forms a pendant, usually from a cumulonimbus cloud, nearly always starts as a funnel cloud and is accompanied by a loud roaring noise.

8.2.3.3.2. Funnel Cloud. A violent, rotating column of air that does not touch the surface. It is usually in the form of a pendant from a cumulonimbus cloud.

8.2.3.3.3. Waterspout. A violent, rotating column of air that forms (or moves) over a body of water and touches the water's surface.

8.2.3.4. Sandstorm (SS). Particles of SA that are carried aloft by a strong wind. The SA particles are mostly confined to the lowest 10 feet, and rarely rise more than 50 feet above the ground.

8.2.3.5. Duststorm (DS). A severe weather condition characterized by strong winds and DU-filled air over an extensive area.

8.2.4. Qualifiers. Intensity. The intensity of weather phenomena is reported using symbols to denote light (-), moderate (no symbol) or heavy (+). **Chapter 13** provides further guidance on which intensity qualifiers can be used with each weather phenomena.

8.2.5. Proximity. Unless directed elsewhere in this document (e.g., reporting the location of thunderstorms and lightning), the proximity qualifier "vicinity" (VC) will be used to identify the location of weather relative to the official point of observation expressed in statute miles. The location of weather phenomena may be reported as "occurring at the station" if within 5 statute miles of the point of observation; "in the vicinity of the station" if between 5 and 10 statute miles of the point of observation; and "distant from the station" (DSNT) when beyond 10 statute miles of the point of observation.

8.2.6. Descriptors. These qualifiers further describe weather phenomena and can be used with certain types of precipitation and obscurations. The terms used are shallow, partial, patches, low drifting, blowing, shower(s), thunderstorm and freezing.

8.2.6.1. Shallow (MI). The descriptor MI is only used to further describe fog that has little vertical extent (less than 6 feet).

8.2.6.2. Partial (PR) and Patches (BC). The descriptors PR and BC is used to further describe fog that has little vertical extent (normally greater than or equal to 6 feet but less than 20 feet), and reduces horizontal visibility, but to a lesser extent vertically. The stars may often be seen by night and the sun by day. PR indicates a phenomenon that covers a substantial portion of the station while BC indicates a phenomenon that randomly covers portions of the station.

8.2.6.3. Low Drifting (DR). A term used to further describe the weather phenomenon when dust, sand or snow is raised by the wind to less than 6 feet.

8.2.6.4. Blowing (BL). A term used to further describe the weather phenomenon when dust, sand, snow and/or spray are raised by the wind to heights 6 feet or greater.

8.2.6.5. Shower(s) (SH). Precipitation characterized by its sudden starting/stopping, rapid change in intensity and accompanied by rapid changes in the appearance of the sky.

8.2.6.6. Thunderstorm (TS). A local storm produced by a cumulonimbus cloud that is accompanied by lightning and/or thunder. Note: Due to the various types of thunderstorm/lightning sensors employed on AF AMOSs, thunderstorm/lightning detection and ranging capability differs from platform to platform (e.g., FMQ-19, TMQ-53, FMQ-22). Weather technicians should review the Lightning Detection Technique and Procedure available on the Air Force Weather Agency Confluence web site, as well as the technical order or operations manual of the AMOS used to gain situational awareness about the capabilities/limitations of these sensors and the need to supplement sensed data from stand-alone sensors with data from a networked lightning detection system and/or other reliable sources (when available).

8.2.6.7. Freezing (FZ). FZ will be used to describe RA or DZ that falls in liquid form but freezes upon impact to form a coating of glaze ice upon the ground and on exposed objects.

8.2.6.8. Freezing Fog (FZFG). When FG is present and the temperature is below 0 degrees C, the descriptor FZ will be used to describe the phenomena. FZFG is a suspension of numerous minute ice crystals in the air or water droplets at temperatures below 0°C and visibility less than 5/8 statute miles, based at the earth's surface. A report of FZFG does not necessarily mean that ice is forming on surfaces.

8.3. Present Weather Alogorithms for AMOS. AMOSs report the type and intensity of precipitation, times of beginning and ending of precipitation, precipitation accumulation and obscurations. **Table 8.1** indicates the types of weather and obscurations generally reported by AMOSs.

8.4. Qualifiers. Intensity and Proximity Qualifier.

8.4.1. Intensity. AMOSs will encode and report light (-), moderate (no symbol), and heavy (+) intensities with all reportable precipitation types except Unknown Precipitation, which is reported as UP.

8.4.2. Proximity. Used only with thunderstorms (TS). With the lightning sensor enabled, AMOSs will report TS as "occurring at the station" if the lightning sensor detects cloud-to-ground strikes within 5 nautical miles of the point of observation, and "in the vicinity of the station" (VCTS) if between 5 and 10 nautical miles of the point of observation. Cloud to ground lightning strikes detected beyond 10 but less than 30 nautical miles are reported in remarks as LTG DSNT followed by the direction.

Table 8.1. Automated Present Weather Reporting

Type	Reporting Notation
Vicinity	VC (used with TS only)
Thunderstorm	TS
Freezing	FZ
Unknown Precipitation	UP (not reported by TMQ-53)
Drizzle	-DZ, DZ, +DZ
Freezing Drizzle	-FZDZ, FZDZ, +FZDZ
Rain	-RA, RA, +RA
Freezing Rain	-FZRA, FZRA, +FZRA
Snow	-SN, SN, +SN
Mist	BR
Fog	FG
Freezing Fog	FZFG
Haze	HZ
Squall	SQ

8.5. Determining Standards. Weather is reported in the body of the observation only when it is detected at the station at the time the observation is prepared for dissemination.

8.5.1. Obscurations. Obscurations are reported in the body of the observation only when they are occurring at the station at the time the observation and the surface visibility is less than 7 statute miles (9999 meters). Other data pertaining to weather and obscurations may be reported in remarks, (e.g., time of beginning/ending of weather). **Note:** Precipitation can also restrict visibility to less than 7 SM without an obscuration present.

8.5.2. Precipitation Occurrence. Precipitation is considered to be occurring when it is accumulating at a rate of at least 0.01 inch/hour (liquid equivalent).

8.5.3. The intensity of precipitation is identified as light, moderate, or heavy IAW one of the following:

8.5.3.1. Intensity of Liquid and Freezing Precipitation. AMOSs determine intensity from particle size and fall velocity through the sensor field. Intensities derived are functionally equivalent to those obtained from the manual rate-of-fall method.

8.5.3.2. Intensity of Snow. When SN is occurring alone, the intensity of SN is based on the reported surface visibilities listed in Table 8.2 If occurring with other precipitation or obscurations, the intensity assigned will be no greater than that determined using the visibility criteria if SN was occurring alone. With or without other obscuring phenomena, AMOSs will not report heavy snow (+SN) if the visibility is greater than 1/4 mile, nor will it report moderate snow (SN) if the visibility is greater than 1/2 mile.

Table 8.2. Intensity of Snow or Drizzle Based on Visibility

Intensity	Criteria
Light	Visibility > 1/2 mile (800 meters).
Moderate	Visibility > 1/4 mile (0400 meters) but ≤ 1/2 mile (800 meters).
Heavy	Visibility ≤ 1/4 mile (0400 meters).

8.5.4. Reporting Beginning and Ending Times of Precipitation. The time precipitation begins or ends is reported in remarks of all observations up to, and including, the next METAR. Times for separate periods of the same type of precipitation (e.g., RA, SN) are reported only if the intervening time of no precipitation exceeds 15 minutes. The format for the remark is given in **Attachment 3.**

8.5.5. Other Weather Phenomena. Other weather phenomena meeting the definitions in **paragraph 8.2** will be measured and reported when observed.

8.6. Manual Observing Methods.

8.6.1. Intensity. Each intensity is defined with respect to the type of precipitation occurring. Use **Table 8.4** to estimate the intensity of RA or FZRA. Use **Table 8.3** to estimate the intensity of PL. Use **Table 8.4** to estimate the intensity of RA or PL using rate of fall. Use **Table 8.2** to estimate the intensity of SN, DZ or FZDZ based on visibility. **Note:** These intensities are based on visibility at the time of observation. When more than one form of precipitation is occurring at a time or precipitation is occurring with an obscuration, the intensities determined will be no greater than that which would be determined if any of the forms were occurring alone.

Table 8.3. Estimating Intensity of Ice Pellets

Intensity	Criteria
Light	Scattered pellets that do not completely cover an exposed surface regardless of duration; visibility is not affected.
Moderate	Slow accumulation on ground; visibility reduced by ice pellets to less than 7 statute miles (9999 meters).
Heavy	Rapid accumulation on ground; visibility reduced by ice pellets to less than 3 statute miles (4800 meters).

Table 8.4. Intensity of Rain or Ice Pellets Based on Rate-of-Fall

Intensity	Criteria
Light	Up to 0.10-inches per hour; maximum 0.01-inch in 6 minutes.
Moderate	0.11-inches to 0.30-inches per hour; more than 0.01-inch to 0.03-inches in 6 minutes.
Heavy	More than 0.30-inches per hour; more than 0.03-inches in 6 minutes.

8.6.2. Precipitation. Augmented stations will report all types of precipitation in the body of the report when they are observed.

8.6.3. Augmented stations will report all other weather phenomena in the body of the report when it is observed. Tornadoes/Waterspouts/Funnel Clouds should only be reported when they are observed by a position-qualified weather technician.

8.6.4. Thunderstorm. A thunderstorm with or without precipitation will be reported in the body or remarks of the observation when observed to begin, be in progress or to end. Remarks concerning the location, movement and direction (if known) of the storm may be added to the METAR/SPECI that reported the thunderstorm.

8.6.4.1. For reporting purposes, a thunderstorm is considered to have begun and to be occurring "at the station" when (1) thunder is first heard when location is unknown, (2) when hail is falling or lightning is observed at or near the airfield and the local noise level is such that resulting thunder cannot be heard or (3) lightning detection equipment indicates lightning strikes within 5 nautical miles of the airfield.

8.6.4.2. When thunder is heard and the location is known (e.g., determined by radar or lighting detector), VCTS may be reported if the location of the storm is determined to be between 5-10 nautical miles. If thunder is heard and the location is determined to be beyond 10-nautical miles, do not carry TS or VCTS in present weather, technicians may include TS comments in remarks (e.g., "TS 12SE MOV NE").

8.6.4.3. A thunderstorm is considered to have ended 15 minutes after the last occurrence of any of the criteria in **paragraph 8.6.4.1**

8.6.5. Beginning/Ending Times for Tornadic Activity, Thunderstorms and Hail. If the initial SPECI taken for the beginning and/or ending of tornadic activity, thunderstorm or hail was not transmitted longline, include the time of beginning (B) and/or ending (E) with the current (most recent) remark in the next SPECI or METAR observation transmitted longline.

8.7. Other Significant Weather Phenomena Reported. Weather technicans should be alert for and may report weather phenomena that are visible from but not occurring at the observing location. Examples are fog banks, localized rain and snow blowing over runways.

Chapter 9

SKY CONDITION

9.1. Introduction. This chapter describes the standards and procedures for automated and manually reporting of sky condition in METAR/SPECI reports.

9.2. Definitions. The following are simple definitions related to sky condition:

9.2.1. Sky Condition. A description of the sky as seen from the surface of the earth.

9.2.2. Horizon. For aviation observation purposes, the actual lower boundary (local horizon) of the observed sky or the upper outline of terrestrial objects, including nearby natural obstructions such as trees and hills. It is the distant line along which the earth (land and or water surface) and the sky appear to meet. The local horizon is based on the best practical points of observation, near the earth's surface, which have been selected to minimize obstruction by nearby buildings, towers, etc.

9.2.3. Celestial Dome. That portion of the sky, which would be visible, provided there was an unobstructed view (due to the absence of buildings, hydrometeors, lithometeors, etc.) of the horizon in all directions from the observation site.

9.2.4. Cloud. A visible accumulation of minute water droplets or ice particles in the atmosphere above the earth's surface. Clouds differ from ground fog, fog, or ice fog only in that the latter are, by definition, in contact with the earth's surface.

9.2.5. Layer. Clouds or obscuring phenomena (not necessarily all of the same type) with bases at approximately the same level. It may be either continuous or composed of detached elements. A trace of cloud or obscuration aloft is always considered as a layer. However, a surface-based obscuring phenomenon is classified as a layer only when it hides 1/8th or more of the sky. If present, a partly obscured condition is always considered to be the lowest layer.

9.2.6. Layer Height. The height of the bases of each reported layer of clouds and/or obscurations. It can also be the vertical visibility into an indefinite ceiling.

9.2.7. Interconnected Cloud Layers. The condition in which cumuliform clouds develop below other clouds and reach or penetrate them. Also, by horizontal extension, swelling cumulus or cumulonimbus may form stratocumulus, altocumulus or dense cirrus.

9.2.8. Summation Principle. The basis on which sky cover classifications are made. This principle states that the sky cover at any level is equal to the summation of the sky cover of the lowest layer plus the additional sky cover present at all successively higher layers up to and including the layer being considered. No layer can be assigned a sky cover less than a lower layer and no sky cover can be greater than 8/8ths. This concept applies to evaluating total sky cover as well as determining ceiling layer.

9.2.9. Ceiling. The lowest layer aloft reported as broken or overcast or the vertical visibility into an indefinite ceiling. If the sky is totally obscured, the vertical visibility will be the ceiling.

9.2.10. Sky Cover. The amount of the sky hidden by clouds and/or obscuration phenomena. This includes cloud cover or obscuring phenomena which hides the sky, but through which the sun or moon (not stars) may be dimly visible. Sky Cover Amounts:

9.2.10.1. Layer Sky Cover. The amount of sky cover at a given level, estimated to the nearest 1/8th.

9.2.10.2. Total Sky Cover. The total amount of sky covered by all layers present. This amount cannot be greater than 8/8ths.

9.2.11. Sky Cover Classifications. The terms used to reflect the degree of cloudiness in sky condition evaluations based on a summation of the amount cloud cover or obscuring phenomena at and below the level of a layer aloft. The basic classification terms are as follows:

9.2.11.1. Clear. A term used to describe the absence of clouds or obscuring phenomena. Clear skies are encoded as **CLR** at automated and augmented locations.

9.2.11.2. Few. A summation sky cover of a trace through 2/8ths. Note that a trace of cloud or obscuration aloft is considered as 1/8th when it is the lowest layer. Encoded as **FEW**.

9.2.11.3. Scattered. A summation sky cover of 3/8ths through 4/8ths. Encoded as **SCT**.

9.2.11.4. Broken. A summation sky cover of 5/8ths through less than 8/8ths. More than 7/8ths but less than 8/8ths is considered as 7/8ths for reporting purposes. Encoded as **BKN**.

9.2.11.5. Overcast. A summation sky cover of 8/8ths. Encoded as **OVC**.

9.2.11.6. Totally Obscured. A condition in which surface-based obscuring phenomena (e.g., fog or snow) are hiding 8/8ths of the sky. The term *indefinite ceiling* may also be used in relation to this sky condition.

9.2.11.7. Partly Obscured. A condition in which surface-based obscuring phenomena are hiding at least 1/8th, but less than 8/8ths, of the sky or higher layers.

9.2.12. Surface. For layer height determinations, the term denotes the horizontal plane whose elevation above mean sea level equals the field elevation. At observing locations where the field elevation has not been established, the term refers to the ground elevation at the observation site.

9.2.13. Variable Ceiling. A condition in which the height of the ceiling layer rapidly increases and decreases during the period of evaluation and the ceiling layer is below 3,000 feet.

9.2.14. Variable Sky Condition. A condition in which a layer height below 3,000 feet that varies between one or more reportable values (FEW, SCT, BKN, OVC) during the period of observation.

9.2.15. Vertical Visibility. A term used to indicate the greatest distance that weather technicians can see vertically upward into an obscuring phenomena or the height corresponding to the upper limit of a laser beam ceilometer's reading.

9.3. Sky Condition Algorithms for AMOS. An AMOS derives sky condition by detecting the frequency and height of clouds passing over the sensor (ceilometer) over a period of 30 minutes. The data from the sensor is processed into layers, amounts, heights and variability of clouds. AMOSs report sky condition from 100 feet up to a maximum of 25,000 feet with the exception of ASOS which will only report to 12,000. AMOSs do not report sky condition above the range of the sensor.

9.4. Determining Standards.

9.4.1. Sky Cover. All sensor output of clouds or obscuring phenomena aloft is considered to be opaque sky cover.

9.4.2. Height of Sky Cover. The laser-beam ceilometer is used to measure the height of layers aloft or the vertical visibility into obscuring phenomena.

9.4.3. Non-Uniform Sky Condition. At AMOS locations that have multiple ceilometers, the data from the meteorological discontinuity sensors are examined and compared with the data from the primary sensor to determine if remarks are required to report non-uniform conditions. The format for the remark is given in **Attachment 3**.

9.4.4. Layer Amounts. Layer amounts are measured according to the reportable values in **Table 9.1**

Table 9.1. Reportable Values for Sky Cover Amount

Reportable Contraction	Meaning	Summation Amount of Layer
VV	Vertical Visibility	8/8
CLR (see Note)	Clear	0
FEW	Few	Trace - 2/8
SCT	Scattered	3/8 - 4/8
BKN	Broken	5/8 - 7/8
OVC	Overcast	8/8
NOTE: The abbreviation **CLR** is used at automated locations when no clouds at or below 12,000 feet are reported (or 25,000 feet with the 25K algorithm) and is used at augmented stations when no layers are reported.		

9.4.5. Layer Heights. Heights of layers are measured in hundreds of feet above the ground, rounded to the nearest reportable increment. Cloud layers from the surface to 5,000 feet are measured to the nearest 100 feet, to the nearest 500 feet for layers from > 5,000 feet to 10,000 feet, and to the nearest 1,000 feet for layers > 10,000 feet. When a value falls halfway between two reportable increments, the lower value is reported.

9.4.6. Variable Ceiling. A ceiling is considered variable when it meets the criteria in Table 9.2. When a variable ceiling, as defined in paragraph 9.2., is detected, it will be reported in the remarks IAW **Attachment 3**.

Table 9.2. Criteria for Variable Ceiling

Ceiling (feet)	Variation Amount (feet)
≤ 1,000	≥ 200
> 1,000 and ≤ 2,000	≥ 400
> 2,000 and < 3,000	≥ 500

9.4.7. Sky cover and ceiling heights from local PIREPS should be used to maintain situational awareness and to compare against the local AMOS or other digital instrumentation. Convert cloud bases reported in PIREPs above mean sea level (MSL) to above ground level (AGL) before comparing to the local data. Reevaluate sky cover and ceiling heights upon receipt of local pilot reports indicating an operationally significant deviation from the current observation.

9.5. Manual Observing Methods. The *WMO International Cloud Atlas*, Volume II, and *Cloud Types for Observers* (available from 14WS) contain detailed guidance and photographs for identifying the various cloud forms.

9.6. Manual Observing Procedures. Sky condition will be evaluated in all METAR and SPECI observations. Weather technicians will evaluate all clouds and obscurations that are visible.

9.6.1. Sky Cover Layers. All layers visible from the observing location should be considered in sky cover reports. A maximum of six layers will be reported in the observation consistent with the priority for reporting layers provided in **Table 13.4**. The report will be based on the eighths (or oktas) of sky covered by each layer in combination with any lower layers. The amount of sky cover for each layer will be the eighths of sky cover attributable to clouds or obscurations (e.g., smoke, haze, fog) in the layer being evaluated. Cloud layers composed of cumulonimbus or towering cumulus may be identified by appending the contractions CB and TCU, respectively to the sky condition. When CB or TCU is appended to the layer report accompanied by the remark (e.g., TCU NW or CB NW MOV E), it is implied that the CB or TCU is associated with the layer and within 10 statute miles. When CB or TCU is outside 10 statute miles, a DSNT remark may be used (e.g., TCU DSNT NW). In this case, CB or TCU would not be appended to the layer in the body of the METAR.

9.6.1.1. Mentally divide the sky into halves or quarters and estimate the layer amount in eighths in each section. Add the total amount of eighths estimated from each quadrant to arrive at a celestial dome coverage estimate. The inverse of this procedure can be done by estimating the amount of clear sky. Subtract this amount from 8/8ths to obtain an estimate of layer coverage.

9.6.1.2. To estimate the amount of an advancing (or receding) layer which extends to the horizon, determine the angular elevation above the horizon of the forward or rear edge of the layer as seen against the sky. Convert the angle to a sky cover amount using Table 9.3 When the layer does not extend to the horizon, determine the angular elevation of the forward and rear edges and the eighths of sky cover corresponding to each elevation angle. The difference will equal the actual sky cover.

9.6.1.3. To estimate the amount of a continuous layer surrounding the observing location and extending to the horizon, determine the angular elevation of the edge of the layer and convert it to a sky cover amount using **Table 9.3** This method is most useful in determining the amount of sky hidden for a partly obscured condition.

Table 9.3. Sky Cover Evaluation

Angle of Advancing or Receding Layer Edge	Eighths of Sky Cover	Angular Elevation of Layer Surrounding Flight
> 0 to 50 degrees	1	> 0 to 10 degrees
51 to 68 degrees	2	11 to 17 degrees
69 to 82 degrees	3	18 to 24 degrees
83 to 98 degrees	4	25 to 32 degrees
99 to 112 degrees	5	33 to 41 degrees
113 to 129 degrees	6	42 to 53 degrees
130 to 179 degrees	7	54 to 89 degrees
180 degrees	8	90 degrees

9.6.2. Evaluation of Interconnected Layers. Clouds formed by the horizontal extension of swelling cumulus or cumulonimbus, that are attached to a parent cloud, will be regarded as a separate layer only if their bases appear horizontal and at a different level from the parent cloud. Otherwise, the entire cloud system will be regarded as a single layer at a height corresponding to the base of the parent cloud.

9.6.3. Cumuliform clouds tend to produce a packing effect. The packing effect occurs when the sides and tops of the clouds are visible, making clouds appear more numerous toward the horizon (see **Figure 9.1** for an illustration of this effect). Estimate layers of sky cover based on the amount of sky actually covered (e.g., to include both the base and sides of the cloud or obscuration).

Figure 9.1. Illustration of Packing Effect

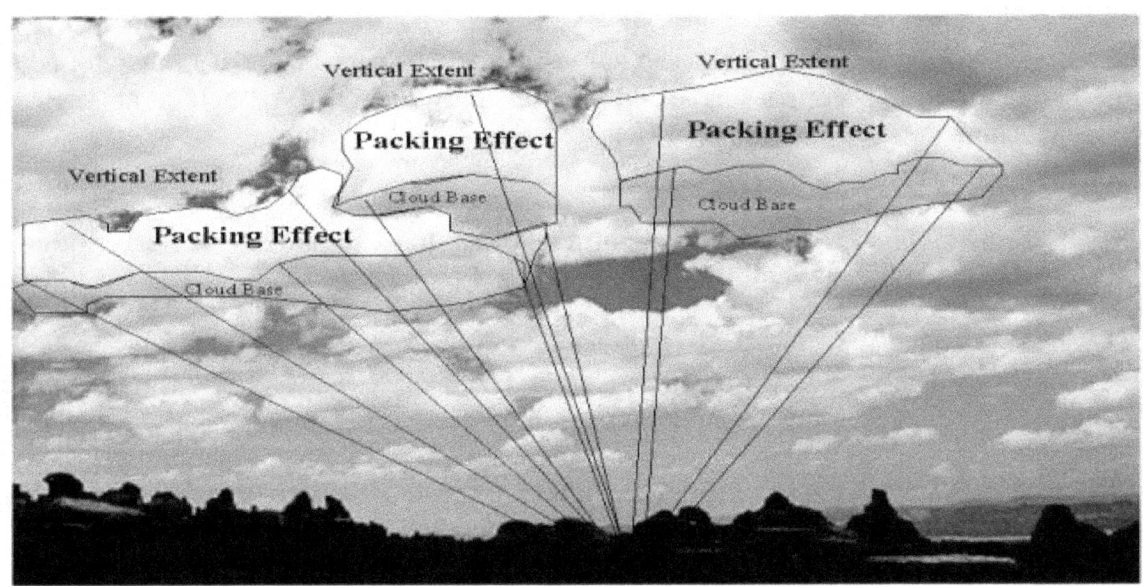

9.6.4. Summation Layer Amount. The summation amount for any given layer is equal to the sum of the sky cover for the layer being evaluated plus the sky cover of all lower layers including partial obscurations. Portions of layers aloft detected through lower layers aloft will not increase the summation amount of the higher layer. A summation amount for a layer cannot exceed 8/8ths. See Table 9.4 for examples of sky condition summation.

Table 9.4. Examples of Sky Condition Summation

Sky Cover Layer	Summation	Sky Condition	Remarks
3/8 obscured by fog	3/8	SCT000	FG SCT000
5/8 stratus at 1,000 feet (3/8 of which are obscured by fog)	5/8	SCT000 BKN010	FG SCT000
2/8 stratocumulus at 4,000 feet	7/8	SCT000 BKN010 BKN040	FG SCT000
Less than 1/8 stratus fractus at 500 feet	1/8	FEW005	
1/8 stratus at 2,000 feet	1/8	FEW005 FEW020	
4/8 cumulonimbus at 3,000 feet	5/8	FEW005 FEW020 BKN030CB	CB W MOV E
8/8 altostratus at 9,000 feet	8/8	FEW005 FEW020 BKN030CB OVC090	CB W MOV E
2/8 smoke at 500 feet	2/8	FEW005	FU FEW005
Indefinite ceiling obscured by snow, vertical visibility 1,000 feet	8/8	FEW005 VV010	FU FEW005

9.6.5. Layer Height. A ceilometer will be used to measure the height of layers aloft. The height of a layer will be the average height of the cloud bases or obscurations for the evaluated layer. Additional ceiling height methods include:

9.6.5.1. AN/TMQ-53, Tactical Meteorological Observing System, or other deployable meteorological equipment.

9.6.5.2. Laser Range Finder. This device must be held as perpendicular to the ground as possible and used only to measure cloud bases directly overhead. If held at an angle, it will display cloud bases at a height greater than the actual height.

9.6.5.3. PIREPs.

9.6.5.4. Known heights of unobscured portions of natural landmarks or objects within 1 1/2 statute miles (2400 meters) from the airfield.

9.6.5.5. Ascension rate of a ceiling balloon.

9.6.5.6. Use of Convective Cloud-Base Height Table. Use **Table 9.5.** only to estimate the height of cumulus clouds formed in the vicinity of your observing location. It cannot be used at observing locations in mountainous or hilly terrain, or to determine the height of other than cumulus clouds. This diagram is most accurate when used to determine the height of cloud bases below 5,000 feet. Use the dry-bulb temperature and dew point to obtain the height of cloud bases above the point of observation.

Table 9.5. Convective Cloud Height Estimates

CONVECTIVE CLOUD-BASE HEIGHT TABLE			
Dewpoint Depression (°C)	Estimated Cloud Base Height (ft)	Dewpoint Depression (°C)	Estimated Cloud Base Height (ft)
0.5	200	10.5	4,200
1.0	400	11.0	4,400
1.5	600	11.5	4,600
2.0	800	12.0	4,800
2.5	1,000	12.5	5,000
3.0	1,200	13.0	5,200
3.5	1,400	13.5	5,400
4.0	1,600	14.0	5,600
4.5	1,800	14.5	5,800
5.0	2,000	15.0	6,000
5.5	2,200	15.5	6,200
6.0	2,400	16.0	6,400
6.5	2,600	16.5	6,600
7.0	2,800	17.0	6,800
7.5	3,000	17.5	7,000
8.0	3,200	18.0	7,200
8.5	3,400	18.5	7,400
9.0	3,600	19.0	7,600
9.5	3,800	19.5	7,800
10.0	4,000	20.0	8,000

9.6.5.7. The apparent size of cloud elements, rolls or features visible in the layer. Large rolls or elements greater than 5 degrees wide (three fingers is about 5 degrees when at arm's length) usually indicate the layer is relatively low. Small rolls or elements between 1 and 5 degrees wide (the little finger is about 1 degree wide when at arm's length) usually indicate the layer is relatively high.

9.6.5.8. The reflection of city or other lights at night can be used. At night, lights may reflect off the base of a layer. This could help estimate the layer's height. For example, a cloud layer over a city may be noticeably illuminated when the base is 5,000 feet or lower. However, a layer may be 1,000 feet or lower for any appreciable illumination from a small town.

Chapter 10

TEMPERATURE AND DEW POINT

10.1. Introduction. This chapter contains standards for measuring temperature and dew point in observations. Defines maximum and minimum temperature and prescribes appropriate observing standards. Dew point and relative humidity are calculated with respect to water at all temperatures.

10.2. Definitions. The following are simple definitions used for determining temperature and dew point:

10.2.1. Air Temperature. A measure of the average kinetic energy of air molecules. It is commonly measured according to the Fahrenheit and Celsius scales.

10.2.2. Dew Point. The temperature to which a given parcel of air must be cooled at constant pressure and constant water vapor content in order for saturation to occur.

10.2.3. Dry-bulb Temperature. The dry-bulb temperature is the ambient temperature that is registered by the dry-bulb thermometer of a psychrometer. It is identical to standard air temperature and may also be used in that sense.

10.2.4. Wet-bulb Temperature. The temperature an air parcel would have if cooled adiabatically to saturation at constant pressure by evaporation of water into it, all latent heat being supplied by the parcel. It differs from the dry-bulb temperature by an amount dependent on the moisture content of the air and, therefore, is generally the same as or lower than the dry-bulb temperature.

10.2.5. Relative Humidity. The ratio, expressed as a percentage, of the actual vapor pressure of the air to the saturation vapor pressure.

10.2.6. Wet-Bulb Depression. The mathematical difference between the dry- and wet-bulb temperatures.

10.3. Temperature/Dew Point Algorithms for AMOS. The AMOS measures temperature and dew point in degrees Celsius. The maximum and minimum temperatures are based on the highest and lowest average temperatures during the period of evaluation. **Note:** The AN/FMQ-19 stops reporting dew point temperatures when the temperature is ≤ -34 degrees Celsius.

10.4. Determining Standards.

10.4.1. Temperature and Dew Point. Temperature and dew point are determined using an AMOS or other digital instrumentation. If no digital method is available, use any backup means available.

10.4.2. Maximum and Minimum Temperature. The maximum and minimum temperatures that occurred in the previous 6 hours are determined and reported to the nearest tenth of a degree Celsius for the 0000, 0600, 1200, and 1800 UTC observations. The maximum and minimum temperatures for the previous 24 hours are determined and reported for the MIDNIGHT (0000 LST) observation. See **Attachment 3** for coding of 6-hourly temperature data.

10.4.3. Units of Measure and Resolution for Temperature and Dew Point. Temperatures and dew point are measured in degrees Celsius, to the nearest whole degree in the body of the report and to the nearest tenth of a degree in the remarks section.

10.5. Manual Observing Methods. For aircraft operations, temperature data is required in reference to the airfield runways. Normally, data measured at another location on the airfield are sufficiently representative of the temperature over the runway.

10.5.1. Observation Periods.   Air and dew point temperatures are reported in each METAR, SPECI, and full element LOCAL observation. Maximum and minimum temperatures, where appropriate, are normally determined at 6-hourly synoptic times and midnight LST.

10.5.2. Determination of Air and Dew point Temperatures.   Obtain air and dew point temperatures by direct reading of the sensors from an AMOS or other digital sensor. If no digital method is available, use any backup means available.

10.5.3. Maximum and Minimum Temperatures. The maximum and minimum temperatures are the highest and the lowest temperature values respectively for a particular day. Determine maximum and minimum temperature extremes of the day from digital readout or temperature recording equipment. If none are available, use the air temperature entries from column 7 of the AF 3803 (24-hour observing locations only).

Chapter 11

PRESSURE

11.1. Introduction. This chapter describes the standards and procedures for determining the various forms of atmospheric pressure and contains instructions for making routine pressure determinations and instrument comparisons. In this chapter, the term "barometric pressure" refers to the actual pressure sensor value. Weather technicians will operate and use all pressure-measuring instruments according to the appropriate T.O. and/or operating manuals. Do not use any pressure-measuring instrument with known or suspected erroneous indications.

11.2. Definitions. Definitions of standard pressure parameters.

11.2.1. Altimeter Setting (A). Altimeter setting defines the pressure value to which an aircraft altimeter scale is set so that the altimeter indicates the altitude above mean sea level of an aircraft on the ground at the location for which the value was determined. This value may be converted from inches of mercury to hPa using **Table 11.7.**, rounding the value down to the nearest whole hPa. **Note:** Q is used at some overseas locations to identify altimeter.

11.2.2. Atmospheric Pressure. The pressure exerted by the atmosphere at a given point.

11.2.3. Barometric Pressure. The atmospheric pressure measured by a barometer.

11.2.4. Density Altitude (DA). The pressure altitude corrected for virtual temperature deviations from the standard atmosphere.

11.2.5. Field Elevation (Ha). The officially designated elevation of an airfield/site above mean sea level. It is the elevation of the highest point on any of the runways of the airfield/site.

11.2.6. Station Elevation (Hp). The officially designated height above sea level to which station pressure pertains. It is generally the same as field elevation.

11.2.7. Non-deployable Barometer. A barometer tasked for use as the primary pressure instrument at a permanent-type site and not intended for deployment.

11.2.8. Pressure-Altitude (PA). The altitude, in the standard atmosphere, at which a given pressure will be observed. It is the indicated altitude of a pressure altimeter at an altitude setting of 29.92 inches (1013.2 hPa) of mercury and is therefore the indicated altitude above or below the 29.92 inches constant-pressure surface. **Note:** QNE is used at some overseas locations.

11.2.9. Pressure Falling Rapidly (PRESFR). A fall in station pressure at the rate of 0.06-inch Hg (2.0 hPa) or more per hour with a total fall of at least 0.02-inch Hg (0.7 hPa) at the time of an observation.

11.2.10. Pressure Rising Rapidly (PRESRR). A rise in station pressure at the rate of 0.06-inch Hg (2.0 hPa) or more per hour with a total rise of at least 0.02-inch Hg (0.7 hPa) at the time of observation.

11.2.11. Pressure Tendency. The pressure characteristic and amount of pressure change during a specified period, usually the 3-hour period preceding an observation.

11.2.12. Removal Correction. A value applied to a pressure reading to compensate for the difference in height between the elevation of the pressure instrument and station elevation. To find the removal correction (inches of mercury), multiply the difference in height in feet by 0.001 inch of mercury per foot. The correction in hectopascals is found by multiplying the difference in feet by 0.036 hectopascals per foot. The removal correction is added to the barometric pressure if the barometer is higher than the runway, and subtracted if the barometer is lower than the runway. Once determined, the same removal correction is always added to the indicated barometric pressure unless the barometer is moved.

11.2.13. Sea Level Pressure (SLP). A pressure value obtained by the theoretical reduction of station pressure to sea level. Where the earth's surface is above sea level, it is assumed the atmosphere extends to sea level below the observing location (station) and the properties of the hypothetical atmosphere are related to conditions observed at the unit. **Note:** QFF is used at some overseas locations.

11.2.14. Standard Atmosphere. A hypothetical vertical distribution of the atmospheric temperature, pressure, and density, which by international agreement, is considered representative of the atmosphere for pressure altimeter calibrations and other purposes.

11.2.15. Station Pressure. The atmospheric pressure at the location's assigned station elevation. Upon request, convert station pressure from inches of mercury to hPa using **Table 11.7** and round the value down to the nearest whole hPa. **Note:** QFE is used at some overseas locations.

11.2.16. Deployable Barometer. A pressure-measuring device (regardless of nomenclature) tasked for deployment (mobility), contingencies or exercises.

11.3. Pressure Algorithms for AMOS. The AMOS computes a pressure relative to the field elevation and then based on that value; compute the pressure parameters (e.g., station pressure, altimeter setting, and sea-level pressure). Computations are made each minute. In addition to the pressure parameters, the AMOS also generates pressure change and pressure tendency remarks for possible inclusion in the observations. AMOS pressure sensors are capable of measuring pressure from 17.5 to 32.5 inches of mercury (600 to 1100hPa).

11.4. Units of Measure. In the United States and at military organizations overseas, data is normally expressed with respect to inches of mercury for station pressure and altimeter setting, and with respect to hectopascals (hPa) for sea-level pressure. The common international unit of measure is hPa for all pressure data (one hPa = one millibar). When required for international aviation purposes, provide pressure data in whole hPa (rounding down in disposing of tenths of an hPa). However, until hectopascals are totally accepted in the verbal and written terminology, the term *millibar* may be used interchangeably with hPa. **Table 11.1** gives the units of measure and the resolution for the pressure parameters.

Table 11.1. Units of Measure and Resolution of Pressure Parameters

Parameter	Unit of Measure	Resolution
Station Pressure	Inches of Mercury	0.005 inch
Altimeter Setting	Inches of Mercury	0.01 inch
Sea Level Pressure	Hectopascals	0.1 Hectopascal
Pressure Altitude	Feet	10 feet
Density Altitude	Feet	10 feet

11.5. Determining Standards. Altimeter setting is reported in the body of the observation. Other pressure data such as pressure rising or falling rapidly, sea level pressure and pressure tendency, when reported, are reported in remarks.

11.6. Priority of Instruments. Obtain pressure data for routine observations using an instrument from the following priority list. The listing is based on instrument availability and the assumption the respective instrument is properly calibrated.

11.6.1. AN/FMQ-19, Automatic Meteorological Station.

11.6.2. AN/FMQ-22, Fixed-Base System

11.6.3. Automated Surface Observing System (ASOS).

11.6.4. AN/TMQ-53, Tactical Meteorological Observing System.

11.6.5. Altimeter Setting Indicator (ASI).

11.6.6. Aircraft altimeter.

11.6.7. Hand-held pressure measuring device (e.g., Kestrel®).

11.6.8. Any other AFWA or MAJCOM-approved device. Note: All permanent observing organizations providing direct observing support to flying operations will have a primary pressure measurement instrument (e.g., AN/FMQ-19, AN/TMQ-53, ASOS) and should have a back-up pressure measuring instrument.

11.7. Manual Observing Procedures. All atmospheric pressure measurements are made on the basis of instrumental evaluation. They will vary according to local requirements and the type of equipment used.

11.7.1. Determination of Station Pressure. Determine station pressure as necessary for use in the surface observation and for computation of other pressure or pressure-related data. The following procedures summarize the common steps used to determine station pressure:

11.7.1.1. Obtain a pressure reading from the appropriate instrument.

11.7.1.2. Determine and apply appropriate corrections to the pressure reading (e.g., algebraically add the posted correction to hand-held pressure measuring device).

11.7.1.3. When necessary, convert the corrected pressure reading from hPa to inches of mercury.

11.7.2. Determination of Altimeter Setting. Read directly from the pressure measuring device or compute an altimeter setting based on a current station pressure value using the method of determination applicable to the unit (e.g., pressure reduction computer, reduction constant or altimeter setting table).

11.7.2.1. Determine altimeter settings as necessary for use in surface observations, upon request, and as otherwise necessary to meet local requirements (e.g., as determined through coordination with using agencies). Normally, compute values to the nearest 0.01-inch Hg (e.g., unless required in hPa for international aviation purposes).

11.7.2.2. During periods between record (hourly) observations, determine an altimeter setting at an interval not to exceed 35 minutes since the last determination (during AMOS back-up for pressure values). Report this value (e.g., as a single element LOCAL or in a METAR or SPECI taken within the established time interval) when there has been a change of 0.01 inch Hg (0.3 hPa) or more since the last locally disseminated value.

11.7.2.3. At augmented EUs, the following procedures may be used as an alternative to the requirement specified in **paragraph 11.7.2.2** during periods with limited air traffic or when no ATC personnel are on duty. In such cases, a formal agreement must be established (and reconfirmed annually) with the airfield operations commander and local agencies concerned. The agreement must include the following requirements for updating altimeter settings during periods when this procedure is applicable:

11.7.2.3.1. The ATC agency must ensure weather technicians are notified at least 30 minutes before each aircraft arrival and departure.

11.7.2.3.2. As soon as possible following each notification of aircraft arrival and departure, weather technicians will determine and report a current altimeter setting if the last locally disseminated value was determined more than 30 minutes before the time of notification.

11.7.2.3.3. At locations where an operational ASI is installed in the control tower, the requirement in **paragraph 11.7.2.2** may be considered not applicable provided the control tower is the only ATC agency requiring altimeter settings and ATC personnel routinely check the ASI for accuracy. A formal agreement must be established (and reconfirmed annually) with the airfield commander and the ATC commander or authorized representative to establish the conditions above and to reaffirm the exemption from the requirement in **paragraph 11.7.2.2**

11.7.3. Pressure Tendency. Pressure tendency and amount of change (reported in the Additive Data 5appp group) are computed automatically by the ADS for every 3-hour observation. To determine pressure tendency and amount of change manually, use the following procedures:

11.7.3.1. Determine the pressure tendency character (the "a" in the 5appp group) from the 3-hour trend of the altimeter settings entered in column 12 of AF 3803. Using the code figures in **Table 11.2,** choose the figure which best describes the character of the change from the altimeter trend.

Table 11.2. Pressure Tendency Character

Primary Requirement	Description	Code Figure
Atmospheric pressure now higher than 3 hours ago	Increasing, then decreasing	0
	Increasing, then steady, or increasing then increasing more slowly	1
	Increasing steadily or unsteadily	2
	Decreasing or steady, then increasing; or increasing then increasing more rapidly	3
Atmospheric pressure now same as 3 hours ago	Increasing, then decreasing	0
	Steady	4
	Decreasing, then increasing	5
Atmospheric pressure now lower than 3 hours ago	Decreasing, then increasing	5
	Decreasing, then steady; or decreasing then decreasing more slowly	6
	Decreasing steadily or unsteadily	7
	Steady or increasing, then decreasing; or decreasing then decreasing more rapidly	8

11.7.3.2. Determine the net change in station pressure (the "ppp" in the 5appp group) for the preceding 3 hours to the nearest 0.005-inch by subtracting the current station pressure from the station pressure from 3 hours ago recorded in column 17 of AF 3803. Disregard the +/- sign as it is not significant to determining net change. Use **Table 11.3** to select the code figure that corresponds to the net change. Limited-duty EUs can access the ADS to obtain past pressure information, if available.

11.7.3.3. Consider the 3-hour pressure tendency group (5appp) as indeterminable when any portion of the group is impossible to determine. Annotate the reason for not reporting the group in column 90.

Table 11.3. Amount of Barometric Change in Last 3 Hours

Amount of Rise or Fall											
ppp						ppp					
Code Figure	Inches of Hg	hPa	Code Figure	Inches of Hg	hPa	Code Figure	Inches of Hg	hPa	Code Figure	Inches of Hg	hPa
000	.000	0.0	051	.150	5.1	102	.300	10.2	152	.450	15.2
002	.005	0.2	052	.155	5.2	103	.305	10.3	154	.455	15.4
003	.010	0.3	054	.160	5.4	105	.310	10.5	156	.460	15.6
005	.015	0.5	056	.165	5.6	107	.315	10.7	157	.465	15.7
007	.020	0.7	058	.170	5.8	108	.320	10.8	159	.470	15.9
008	.025	0.8	059	.175	5.9	110	.325	11.0	161	.475	16.1
010	.030	1.0	061	.180	6.1	112	.330	11.2	163	.480	16.3
012	.035	1.2	063	.185	6.3	113	.335	11.3	164	.485	16.4
014	.040	1.4	064	.190	6.4	115	.340	11.5	166	.490	16.6
015	.045	1.5	066	.195	6.5	117	.345	11.7	168	.495	16.8
017	.050	1.7	068	.200	6.8	119	.350	11.9	169	.500	16.9
019	.055	1.9	069	.205	6.9	120	.355	12.0	171	.505	17.1
020	.060	2.0	071	.210	7.1	122	.360	12.2	173	.510	17.3
022	.065	2.2	073	.215	7.3	124	.365	12.4	174	.515	17.4
024	.070	2.4	075	.220	7.5	125	.370	12.5	176	.520	17.6
025	.075	2.5	076	.225	7.6	127	.375	12.7	178	.525	17.8
027	.080	2.7	078	.230	7.8	129	.380	12.9	179	.530	17.9
029	.085	2.9	080	.235	8.0	130	.385	13.0	181	.535	18.1
030	.090	3.0	081	.240	8.1	132	.390	13.2	183	.540	18.3
032	.095	3.2	083	.245	8.3	134	.395	13.4	185	.545	18.5
034	.100	3.4	085	.250	8.5	135	.400	13.5	186	.550	18.6
036	.105	3.6	086	.255	8.6	137	.405	13.7	188	.555	18.8
037	.110	3.7	088	.260	8.8	139	.410	13.9	190	.560	19.0
039	.115	3.9	090	.265	9.0	141	.415	14.1	191	.565	19.1
041	.120	4.1	091	.270	9.1	142	.420	14.2	193	.570	19.3
042	.125	4.2	093	.275	9.3	144	.425	14.4	195	.575	19.5
044	.130	4.4	095	.280	9.5	146	.430	14.6	196	.580	19.6
046	.135	4.6	097	.285	9.7	147	.435	14.7	198	.585	19.8
047	.140	4.7	098	.290	9.8	149	.440	14.9	200	.590	20.0
049	.145	4.9	100	.295	10.0	151	.445	15.1	201	.595	20.1
									203	.600	20.3

NOTE: Code figures in this table are based on the conversion from inches of mercury to hectopascals since station pressure is taken in inches of mercury. However, other code figures not listed (e.g., 016 for 1.6 hPa) are also used at locations where station pressure is determined in hectopascals.

11.7.4. Determination of Pressure Altitude and Density Altitude. Compute PA and DA based on a current station pressure value and the method of determination applicable to the EU (e.g., pressure reduction computer or table for PA, density altitude computer for DA). Determine and report data as necessary to meet locally established requirements, (e.g., in conjunction with each determination of altimeter setting). Compute data to at least the nearest 10 feet. The FMQ-19 and ADS compute density altitude using almost identical formulas, however, the ADS formula takes into account water vapor and the FMQ-19 does not. The differences between the calculations are between 5% and 12%, the ADS calculation being slightly more accurate due to the additional water vapor calculation. Currently, aircrews are instructed to use the "dry" or FMQ-19 computation and then add the water vapor computation, if necessary. AFW organizations should provide the dry DA computation to supported organizations, unless specifically asked to provide a different computation. Advise ATC agencies that PA/DA values are estimated when backing-up of the AMOS pressure sensor.

11.7.5. Determination of Sea-Level Pressure. Compute sea-level pressure (QFF) based on a current station pressure value and the method of determination applicable to the station (pressure reduction computer, reduction constant, or Sea Level Pressure table). Determine QFF values hourly, to the nearest 0.1 hPa. The QFF must be considered as estimated when the 12-hour mean temperature used in computations is based on an estimate of the air temperature 12 hours previously. Limited-duty EUs can access the ADS to obtain past temperature information, if available.

11.7.6. Determination of Significant Pressure Changes. When pressure is falling or rising rapidly at the time of an observation, report the condition in the remarks of the observation. When the pressure is rising or falling at a rate of 0.06-inch Hg per hour or more, totaling a change 0.02-inch Hg or more at the time of observation, the remark PRESRR (pressure rising rapidly) or PRESFR (pressure falling rapidly) will be included in the observation. These conditions may be considered operationally significant and included with an altimeter setting LOCAL or other observation disseminated to ATC personnel.

11.7.7. Estimated Pressure Values. Although all pressure data are instrumentally derived, values must be classified as estimated under certain conditions. The altimeter, station pressure, and all other pressure data will be classified as estimated as follows:

11.7.7.1. Any correction factor is based on an approximation.

11.7.7.2. A scheduled barometer comparison is delayed and the reliability of the previous correction is suspected to be in error by more than 0.020 inch Hg (0.70 hPa). This decision should be as objective as practical and based on such factors as past instrument performance, the length of the delay and the reason for the delay.

11.7.7.3. Anytime pressure readings are suspect in the opinion of weather personnel.

11.7.7.4. When deployable equipment is used as a back-up to the primary pressure measurement instrument. EUs may use the AN/TMQ-53 as back-up without estimating pressure values if the requirements in **paragraph 3.5 – 3.5.3** are met. Pressure values from other deployable meteorological equipment, the sensors from the AN/FMQ-19 discontinuity group (and midfield if available) or other MAJCOM-approved back-up equipment will be estimated.

11.8. Standardization and Comparison Procedures. Each EU with an AN/TMQ-53 and/or hand-held weather device (e.g., Kestrel®) must establish a barometry program. Instructions in the following paragraphs are generally limited to those aspects of barometry required by weather technician in making routine pressure measurements for aviation observations.

11.8.1. Standardization of deployable digital barometers (e.g., AN/TMQ-53, Kestrel®). Deployable barometers will be qualified for operational use. At a minimum, compare digital barometers against a standard barometer annually. Complete a barometer comparison before deployment (when possible) and upon return from a deployment.

11.8.1.1. Set up and operate the equipment IAW the TO and/or the operating manual.

11.8.1.2. Hand-held weather device (e.g., Kestrel®)

11.8.1.2.1. Make a series of at least four comparisons, not less than 15 minutes apart, against the EU standard barometer. Establish a mean correction from the comparisons.

11.8.1.2.2. Apply the mean correction to the pressure readings, or adjust the pressure software to reflect the correction. If the mean correction exceeds 0.020-inch Hg (0.70 hPa), discontinue use and replace the handheld device.

11.8.1.3. AN/TMQ-53. A qualified maintenance technician will calibrate the TMQ-53 pressure sensor initially and seim-annually thereafter, using a standard digital barometer that conforms with the TMQ-53 technical order or OEM pressure sensor specifications.

11.8.1.4. Deployable digital barometers at locations with no EU standard barometer. Compare each deployable barometer against any available calibrated pressure instrument (e.g., aircraft altimeter, collocated NWS/FAA ASI) following the same procedures for locations with a EU standard barometer.

11.8.1.5. Deployed Hand-Held weather device (e.g., Kestrel®)

11.8.1.5.1. Conduct a series of four barometer comparisons against the most reliable calibrated pressure device available (a second deployed barometer or an aircraft altimeter), before first use, daily thereafter, and whenever the device is relocated.

11.8.1.5.2. Determine the mean correction after four comparisons (use only comparisons made at the deployed site); use the mean as the posted correction, and adjust the hand-held weather device IAW the operating manual or T.O.

11.8.1.6. Deployed TMQ-53.

11.8.1.6.1. Conduct a series of four barometer comparison, not less than 15 minutes apart, against the most reliable calibrated pressure device available (a second deployed barometer or an aircraft altimeter), before first use and whenever the device is relocated.

11.8.1.6.2. Determine the mean correction after four comparisons (use only comparisons made at the deployed site). Use the mean as the posted correction and if the difference exceeds 0.01inHG, adjust the AN/TMQ-53 IAW the T.O.

11.8.1.6.3. A qualified maintenance technician will calibrate the TMQ-53 pressure sensor as soon as possible after deployment or relocation, and annually thereafter, using a standard digital barometer that conforms with the TMQ-53 T.O. or OEM pressure sensor specifications.

11.8.1.7. Do not use any pressure measuring instrument with known or suspected erroneous indications.

11.8.2. Altimeter Setting Indicator (ASI). At EUs equipped with and using an ASI, establish a standardization and comparison program based on procedures comparable to those specified for the non-deployable barometer.

11.8.3. Record and document barometer comparisons on a locally developed worksheet/spreadsheet, or MAJCOM or higher headquarters approved form/worksheet/spreadsheat. Retain the last two barometer comparisons on file and dispose all others.

11.9. Pressure Sensor Range. AMOS pressure sensors are capable of measuring pressure from 17.5 to 32.5 inches of mercury (600 to 1100 hectopascals [hPa]).

11.10. Pressure Reporting Standards. Altimeter setting is reported in the body of the observation. Other pressure data, such as PRESRR or PRESFR, SLP and pressure tendency, when reported, are reported in remarks. Report PA/DA values provided to ATC agencies IAW locally derived procedures (e.g., local dissemination log).

11.10.1. Reporting Frequency of Altimeter Setting. Altimeter setting is reported in all observations.

11.10.2. Reporting Frequency of Pressure Remarks. The pressure change remarks (PRESFR, PRESRR) are included in all observations when appropriate. The Sea-Level Pressure is included in the remarks section of all automated observations and required in METARs when in augmented. The pressure tendency remark (5appp) is only included in 3- and 6-hourly observations. The format for these remarks and additive data are given in **Attachment 3.**

Table 11.4. Summary of Pressure Observing and Reporting Standards

Data	AMOS Output
Altimeter Setting	Reported in inches of mercury.
Remarks: - Rising Rapidly - Falling Rapidly - Sea Level Pressure - Tendency	Reported as **PRESRR.** Reported as **PRESFR.** Reported in Hectopascals as **SLPppp.** Reported as **5appp. (Note:** AMOSs report pressure net change code figures that **Table 11.4.** may not reflect, e.g., 001, 004, 006, 011, etc.).

11.11. Deployed Operations. Deployed EUs may use the AN/TMQ-53 without estimating pressure values if conditions in **paragraph 3.5. - 3.5.3** are met.

11.12. Equipment Operation and Instrument Evaluation.

11.12.1. General.   Operate and use all pressure-measuring instruments according to the appropriate TO and/or operating manuals.

11.12.2. Aircraft Altimeter.   In the event an aircraft altimeter is the only instrument available, it may be used in obtaining estimated pressure data for the surface observation. Set the altitude scale to indicate the actual elevation of the instrument and take readings to the nearest 0.01-inch Hg.

11.12.3. Pressure Reduction Computer. The following procedures outline requirements in using the pressure reduction computer for computation of pressure data:

11.12.3.1. Altimeter Setting.   Step-by-step procedures are printed on side II of the reduction computer. Compute the altimeter setting using station pressure to the nearest 0.005 inch Hg and station elevation to the nearest foot. If the station pressure is in hectopascals, the value can be readily converted to inches of mercury using the scale on side I of the computer. Table 11.5 provides examples of this process.

Table 11.5. Determine Altimeter Setting

	A	B	C	D
Station Pressure (inches Hg)	29.065	28.820	23.555	30.070
Station Elevation (feet)	763	1238	6545	165
Altimeter setting (inches Hg)	29.88	30.14	30.00	30.25

11.12.3.2. Pressure Altitude.   Side II of the pressure reduction computer contains instructions for determining pressure altitude as a function of station pressure. Use station pressure (to the nearest 0.005-inch Hg) and read the pressure altitude from the computer to at least the nearest 10 feet. Table 11.6 provides examples of this process.

Table 11.6. Determine Pressure Altitude

	A	B	C	D
Station Pressure (inches Hg)	29.065	28.820	23.555	30.070
Corresponding PA (feet)	+800	+1030	+6470	-140

Table 11.7. Conversion of Altimeter Setting From Inches of Mercury to Hectopascals

Inch HG	0.00	0.01	0.02	0.03	0.04	0.05	0.06	0.07	0.08	0.09
	Hectopascals									
28.0	948.2	948.5	948.9	949.2	949.5	949.9	950.2	950.6	950.9	951.2
28.1	951.6	951.9	952.3	952.6	952.9	953.3	953.6	953.9	954.3	954.6
28.2	955.0	955.3	955.6	956.0	956.3	956.7	957.0	957.3	957.7	958.0
28.3	958.3	958.7	959.0	959.4	959.7	960.0	960.4	960.7	961.1	961.4
28.4	961.7	962.1	962.4	962.8	963.1	963.4	963.8	964.1	964.4	964.8
28.5	965.1	965.5	965.8	966.1	966.5	966.8	967.2	967.5	967.8	968.2
28.6	968.5	968.8	969.2	969.5	969.9	970.2	970.5	970.9	971.2	971.6
28.7	971.9	972.2	972.6	972.9	973.2	973.6	973.9	974.3	974.6	974.9
28.8	975.3	975.6	976.0	976.3	976.6	977.0	977.3	977.7	978.0	978.3
28.9	978.7	979.0	979.3	979.7	980.0	980.4	980.7	981.0	981.4	981.7
29.0	982.1	982.4	982.7	983.1	983.4	983.7	984.1	984.4	984.8	985.1
29.1	985.4	985.8	986.1	986.5	986.8	987.1	987.5	987.8	988.2	988.5
29.2	988.8	989.2	989.5	989.8	990.2	990.5	990.9	991.2	991.5	991.9
29.3	992.2	992.6	992.9	993.2	993.6	993.9	994.2	994.6	994.9	995.3
29.4	995.6	995.9	996.3	996.6	997.0	997.3	997.6	998.0	998.3	998.6
29.5	999.0	999.3	999.7	1000.0	1000.4	1000.7	1001.0	1001.4	1001.7	1002.0
29.6	1002.4	1002.7	1003.1	1003.4	1003.7	1004.1	1004.4	1004.7	1005.1	1005.4
29.7	1005.8	1006.1	1006.4	1006.8	1007.1	1007.5	1007.8	1008.1	1008.5	1008.8
29.8	1009.1	1009.5	1009.8	1010.2	1010.5	1010.8	1011.2	1011.5	1011.9	1012.2
29.9	1012.5	1012.9	1013.2	1013.5	1013.9	1014.2	1014.6	1014.9	1015.2	1015.6
30.0	1015.9	1016.3	1016.6	1016.9	1017.3	1017.6	1018.0	1018.3	1018.6	1019.0
30.1	1019.3	1019.6	1020.0	1020.3	1020.7	1021.0	1021.3	1021.7	1022.0	1022.4
30.2	1022.7	1023.0	1023.4	1023.7	1024.0	1024.4	1024.7	1025.1	1025.4	1025.7
30.3	1026.1	1026.4	1026.7	1027.1	1027.4	1027.8	1028.1	1028.4	1028.8	1029.1
30.4	1029.5	1029.8	1030.1	1030.5	1030.8	1031.2	1031.5	1031.8	1032.2	1032.5
30.5	1032.9	1033.2	1033.5	1033.9	1034.2	1034.5	1034.9	1035.2	1035.5	1035.9
30.6	1036.2	1036.6	1036.9	1037.3	1037.6	1037.9	1038.3	1038.6	1038.9	1039.2
30.7	1039.6	1040.0	1040.3	1040.6	1041.0	1041.3	1041.7	1042.0	1042.3	1042.7
30.8	1043.0	1043.3	1043.7	1044.0	1044.4	1044.7	1045.0	1045.4	1045.7	1046.1
30.9	1046.4	1046.7	1047.1	1047.4	1047.8	1048.1	1048.4	1048.8	1049.1	1049.5

NOTE: When provided for use by international aviators, the altimeter setting is rounded down to the nearest whole hectopascal, e.g., 29.14 inches Hg = 986.8 hPa, rounded down to 986 hPa.

Chapter 12

PRECIPITATION MEASUREMENT

12.1. General Information. This chapter contains a description of the methods used to measure precipitation amounts and snow depth.

12.2. Definitions.

12.2.1. Water Equivalent. Term that refers to the liquid water equivalent of a solid form of precipitation that is melted.

12.2.2. Solid Precipitation. Any precipitation that is freezing or frozen (e.g., SN, SG or FZRA).

12.3. Precipitation Algorithms for AMOS.

12.3.1. Precipitation measurements from an AMOS are normally made by heated and non-heated (depending on the system) rain gauges and present weather sensors.

12.3.2. AN/FMQ-19 and AN/TMQ-53 rain gauges have a 0.01" capacity before reporting precipitation amount.

12.3.3. AMOS present weather sensors use infrared light to identify and measure precipitation based on characteristic interference signatures. In addition to using IR to identify and measure precipitation, the TMQ-53 also uses two capacitance sensors to increase sensitivity to very light precipitation (e.g., -DZ). On the TMQ-53, the sensor uses an algorithm to estimate snow depth based on particulate size and rate of fall and uses temperature ranges (using its internal temperature sensor) to assist with the snow depth calculations using different ratios (in essence, "wet/warmer temps", "medium/average" and "dry/cold").

12.4. Determining Standards. The measurement of precipitation is expressed in terms of vertical depth of water (or water equivalent in the case of solid forms) that reaches the surface during a specified period. In METAR observations, requirements for the measurement of precipitation are established to include both liquid and frozen amounts that have fallen and the total depth of solid forms on the ground at the time of observation. **Note:** The term solid is sometimes used as a synonym for frozen forms of precipitation.

12.4.1. Unit of Measurement. The basic unit of measurement is the inch. MAJCOMs or higher headquarters may require EUs to report in millimeters (mm) for liquid precipitation (or water equivalent) and centimeters (cm) for frozen precipitation and snow depth. Table 12.1 provides guidance for converting new snowfall to water equivalent.

12.4.1.1. Liquid precipitation (or water equivalent): To the nearest 0.01". Less than 0.005" is termed a trace.

12.4.1.2. Frozen/Freezing precipitation: To the nearest 0.1". Less than 0.05" is termed a trace.

12.4.1.3. Snow depth (any solid form): To the nearest whole inch. Less than 0.5" is termed a trace.

12.4.2. Observation Periods.   Precipitation and snow depth measurements are normally obtained at 3- and 6-hourly synoptic times and at midnight LST. Make measurements more frequently when necessary to meet local or other support requirements.

12.4.3. Representative Area for Measurement of Solid Forms.   In obtaining samples or measurements of snowfall and depth of snow on the ground, select an area that is smooth, level, preferably grass covered and as free from drifting as possible. Avoid using paved areas and low spots where water tends to collect. Select an area that permits measurements to be taken in undisturbed snow.

12.4.3.1. As an aid in obtaining the measurement of new snowfall, place snowboards on top of the snow after each measurement. The next measurement can then be taken from the top of the snow to the snowboard.

12.4.3.2. The snowboard can be a thin, light-colored wooden board or a thin light-colored, lightweight composite material board (composite material must be a poor conductor of heat). The snowboard must be at least 2'X 2' (about 60 cm) square and should be at least 1/2" thick. Flag or mark snowboards in such a way that it is left undisturbed by non-weather personnel.

12.4.3.3. In using the area, start measurements along the edge nearest the observation location to avoid unnecessary tracking of the snow. Unless the snow is very deep and drifting is pronounced, take a measurement 2' (about 60 cm) from previous measurements.

12.4.3.4. Irregularities (e.g., uneven terrain, drifting and footsteps before sampling) tend to introduce unavoidable errors in the measurements. Therefore, classify amounts as estimated if they are not considered representative.

12.4.4. Measurement of Precipitation Amounts (water equivalent). Water equivalent is an expression used to reflect the amount of liquid produced by the melting of solid forms of precipitation.   Obtain precipitation amounts (or water equivalent) using the following procedures:

12.4.4.1. Under normal circumstances, obtain liquid precipitation amounts and the water equivalent of frozen/freezing precipitation using the collection in the rain gauge.

12.4.4.2. If the rain gauge collection is not considered representative, disregard the catch and classify the amount of precipitation as undeterminable when it consists entirely of liquid types.   If possible, obtain water equivalent by means of core sampling or estimation when precipitation during the period consisted entirely of solid forms.

12.4.4.3. To estimate water equivalent of solid forms of precipitation, first obtain a measurement of the snowfall. Convert the actual depth to its water equivalent based on a 1:10 ratio (or other ratio if known to be representative for the unit or the snowfall). For example, if 1.6 inches of snow has fallen, the water equivalent is approximately 0.16 inch (1.6 divided by 10 = 0.16) in using a 1:10 ratio. For 4 cm (40 mm) of snowfall, the water equivalent is approximately 4 mm in using a 1:10 ratio. Use Table 12.1 to help determine the water equivalent of new snowfall only. Packing and melting/freezing has a substantial effect on the density of the snow pack and is not accounted for in this table.

12.4.5. Measurement of Snowfall (Solid Precipitation). For the purpose of snowfall measurements, the term snow also includes other types of freezing and frozen precipitation that fell during the measurement period. Obtain snowfall amounts using the following procedures as a guide.

12.4.5.1. Using a standard ruler (graduated in inches) or other suitable measuring device, measure the depth in several locations, preferably at points where the snow has fallen and is undisturbed by the wind. If practical, make these measurements using snowboards or a surface that has been cleared of previous snowfall. If the previous snowfall has crusted, the new fall may be measured by permitting the end of the ruler to rest on the crust.

12.4.5.1.1. If a suitable spot is not available and snowboards are not in place, the snowfall amount may be obtained by measuring the total depth of snow and subtracting the depth previously measured. This will normally be estimated due to the effects of melting, sublimation, etc.

12.4.5.1.2. When melting or settling occurred between measurements, estimate the depth of new snow that would have collected if the melting or settling had not occurred. For instance, if several snow showers occur between observations and each melts before the following one occurs, the total snowfall for the period will be the sum of the maximum depth (measured or estimated) for each occurrence.

12.4.5.2. Obtain an average of the several measurements to the nearest 0.1". Consider the amount as estimated if there is any doubt as to its accuracy, (e.g., melting, drifting).

12.4.5.3. When an accurate water equivalent of frozen precipitation has been obtained, the snowfall amount may be estimated based on a 1:10 ratio (or other ratio if known to be representative. For example, if the water equivalent of snowfall from the rain gauge is 0.16 inch, the actual amount of snowfall is approximately 1.6 inches (0.16 times 10 = 1.6) using a 1:10 ratio. If the water equivalent is 4 mm, the actual amount of snowfall is approximately 40 mm (or 4 cm) using the 1:10 ratio.

12.4.6. Measurement of Total Snow Depth. For the purpose of snow depth measurements, the term snow also includes other types of frozen precipitation (e.g., ice pellets, hail) and sheet ice formed directly or indirectly from precipitation. Obtain total depth of snow in conjunction with snowfall measurements using the following procedures:

12.4.6.1. Using a standard ruler or other suitable measuring device, measure the total depth in several locations, preferably at points where the snow is undisturbed by the wind.

12.4.6.1.1. If the ground is covered with ice, cut through the ice with some suitable implement and measure its thickness. Add the thickness of the ice to the depth of snow above the ice.

12.4.6.1.2. When the snow has drifted, include the greatest and least depths in measurements from the representative area. For example, if spots with no snow are visible, use zero as one of the values.

12.4.6.1.3. Obtain an average of the several measurements, to the nearest whole inch.

12.4.6.2. Estimates of total depth may be obtained using snow stakes at observing location where this method is considered necessary and practical. In such cases, place several stakes in the most representative area available, (e.g., where the snow is least likely to be disturbed within a few feet (or meters) of the stakes). Obtain an average depth by reference to graduated markings on the stakes.

Table 12.1. New Snowfall to Water Equivalent Conversion

Melt Water Equivalent (WE) in Inches	New Snowfall (inches) Temperature (°C)						
	01-M02	M03-M07	M07-M09	M10-M12	M13-M18	M18-M29	M30-M40
Trace	Trace	0.1	0.2	0.3	0.4	0.5	1.0
.01	0.1	0.2	0.2	0.3	0.4	0.5	1.0
.02	0.2	0.3	0.4	0.6	0.8	1.0	2.0
.03	0.3	0.5	0.6	0.9	1.2	1.5	3.0
.04	0.4	0.6	0.8	1.2	1.6	2.0	4.0
.05	0.5	0.8	1.0	1.5	2.0	2.5	5.0
.06	0.6	0.9	1.2	1.8	2.4	3.0	6.0
.07	0.7	1.1	1.4	2.1	2.8	3.5	7.0
.08	0.8	1.2	1.6	2.4	3.2	4.0	8.0
.09	0.9	1.4	1.8	2.7	3.6	4.5	9.0
.10	1.0	1.5	2.0	3.0	4.0	5.0	10.0
.11	1.1	1.7	2.2	3.3	4.4	5.5	11.0
.12	1.2	1.8	2.4	3.6	4.8	6.0	12.0
.13	1.3	2.0	2.6	3.9	5.2	6.5	13.0
.14	1.4	2.1	2.8	4.2	5.6	7.0	14.0
.15	1.5	2.3	3.0	4.5	6.0	7.5	15.0
.16	1.6	2.4	3.2	4.8	6.4	8.0	16.0
.17	1.7	2.6	3.4	5.1	6.8	8.5	17.0
.18	1.8	2.7	3.6	5.4	7.2	9.0	18.0
.19	1.9	2.9	3.8	5.7	7.6	9.5	19.0
.20	2.0	3.0	4.0	6.0	8.0	10.0	20.0
.21	2.1	3.1	4.2	6.3	8.4	10.5	21.0
.22	2.2	3.3	4.4	6.6	8.8	11.0	22.0
.23	2.3	3.4	4.6	6.9	9.2	11.5	23.0
.24	2.4	3.6	4.8	7.2	9.6	12.0	24.0
.25	2.5	3.8	5.0	7.5	10.0	12.5	25.0
.30	3.0	4.5	6.0	9.0	12.0	15.0	30.0
.35	3.5	5.3	7.0	10.5	14.0	17.5	35.0
.40	4.0	6.0	8.0	12.0	16.0	20.0	40.0
.45	4.5	6.8	9.0	13.5	18.0	22.5	45.0
WE Ratio	1:10	1:15	1:20	1:30	1:40	1:50	1:100

Melt Water Equivalent (WE) in Inches	New Snowfall (inches) Temperature (°C)						
	01-M02	M03-M07	M07-M09	M10-M12	M13-M18	M18-M29	M30-M40
.50	5.0	7.5	10.0	15.0	20.0	25.0	50.0
.60	6.0	9.0	12.0	18.0	24.0	30.0	60.0
.70	7.0	10.5	14.0	21.0	28.0	35.0	70.0
.80	8.0	12.0	16.0	24.0	32.0	40.0	80.0
.90	9.0	13.5	18.0	27.0	36.0	45.0	90.0
1.00	10.0	15.0	20.0	30.0	40.0	50.0	100.0
2.00	20.0	30.0	40.0	60.0	80.0	100.0	200.0
3.00	30.0	45.0	60.0	90.0	120.0	150.0	300.0
WE Ratio	1:10	1:15	1:20	1:30	1:40	1:50	1:100

Note: For temperatures above 34°F (1°C) or for slushy, wet snow, a 1:8 ratio may be appropriate, e.g., 0.10" WE = 0.8" snowfall, 0.15" WE = 1.2" snowfall.

Table 12.2. Precipitation Reporting Guide for Limited-Duty EUs

This is a guide to assist limited duty weather EUs that do not begin observing until after 1200Z or the MAJCOM specified 24-hour precipitation reporting time for your base. All entries reference the surface weather observation forms.
1. Column 44 (Precipitation Water Equivalent). a. The "Mid To" line on Column 44 has no entry (unless open at midnight LST). b. Column 44 (1-4) has entries, e.g., 0 for no precipitation, T for Trace. c. The "Mid" line on Column 44 has no entry (unless open at midnight LST).
2. Column 45 (Snowfall). a. The "Mid To" line on Column 45 has no entry. b. Column 45 (1-4) has entries, e.g., 0 for no snowfall, T for Trace. c. The "Mid" line on Column 45 has no entry.
3. Column 46 (Snow depth). a. The "Mid To" line on Column 46 has no entry. b. Column 46 (1-4) has entries (nearest whole inch), e.g., 0 for no snow depth, T for Trace (less than a half inch). c. The "Mid" line on Column 46 has no entry.
4. Column 68 (Summary of the Day, Precipitation Water Equivalent).
5. Encode using the sum of blocks 1-4 in Column 44.
6. Column 69 (Summary of the Day, Snowfall).
7. Encode using the sum of blocks 1-4 in Column 45.
8. Column 70 (Summary of the Day, Snow Depth). Enter to nearest whole inch using the measurement taken on the opening observation, e.g., 1400Z.
9. Column 13 Remarks (3- and 6-Hour Precipitation Amount, 6RRRR). a. Encode 6RRR on the first 3- or 6-hourly observation after opening; e.g., station opened at 1400Z then report on the 1500Z observation or station opened at 1600Z report on the 1800Z observation. If the first hour opened is on a 3- or 6- hourly and precipitation is observed, carry 6/////. b. Enter as the sum of precipitation from the opening observation to the first 3- or 6- hourly observation; e.g., station opened at 1400Z then the 6RRRR on the 1500Z observation is one hour of precipitation. c. Continue to encode and report on subsequent 6-hourly observations while open.
10. Column 13 Remarks (24-Hour Precipitation, 7R24R24R24R24). a. If precipitation occurred, encode and report on the first observation of the day (if first observation is between 1 – 2 hours after your 24-hour precipitation (7-group) reporting time (e.g., 1300Z to 1400Z)). If not, or limited observation were taken at other than 1300Z to 1400Z, then report the 7-group on the first 6-hourly METAR after opening. b. Encode and report using the sum of Column 44, lines 2-4 from the previous day and Column 44, line 1 from the current day. c. The 24-Hour Precipitation group will always be reported in increments of 24. For periods longer than 24 hours, encode in Column 13 as ESTMD PCPN, e.g., 96 HR ESTMD PCPN, prefix amount with an asterisk in column 44 and a corresponding remark in Column 90, e.g., *96-HR PCPN. Include the actual time period remark (e.g., 96-HR ESTMD PCPN) in the plain language section of remarks of the longline observation.

11. Reporting precipitation during periods of limited observations (e.g., weekends and holidays) when the airfield is only open for a few hours and may not be open during a scheduled 6-hourly observation.

a. If you are closed during a scheduled 6-hourly observation, but are open during a scheduled 3-hourly observation, encode and report in column 13 of the AF 3803 in the 6RRRR group. Do not dump the rain gauge when this occurs.

b. If you are open between 1200Z-1400Z (or MAJCOM approved 24-hour (7-group) precipitation reporting time) for a scheduled 6-hourly observation, encode and report precipitation appropriately (as stated above). Dump rain gauge at these times always.

12. The weather technician will only dump precipitation from the rain gauge when opening between normal hours (1200Z-1400Z or MAJCOM approved 24-hour (7-group) precipitation reporting time) and subsequent 6-hourly observations. No exceptions.

13. The opening weather technician will always report precipitation extending back to the last 6-hourly observation, whether it was the day before or the entire weekend.

14. The closing weather technician will dump the rain gauge and report precipitation when closing on a scheduled 6-hourly observation, but will never dump or encode/report when closing on non 6-hourly observations (unless at midnight local).

12.5. Manual Observing Methods.

12.5.1. General. Manual precipitation measurements are normally made by means of ML-17 standard 8-inch rain and snow gauge. The ML-217 (a 4-inch plastic gauge) and automatic precipitation measuring devices also are used. For deployed location measurements, use the ML-217, or equivalent. Limited-duty locations will report precipitation according to **Table 12.2**

12.5.2. Installation of the Rain Gauge. Install the rain gauge in the open, away from such obstructions as buildings and trees. Low obstructions (e.g., bushes, walls or fences) are usually beneficial in breaking the force of the wind. However, place the gauge no closer to an obstruction than a distance equal to the height of the object. If the gauge is mounted on top of a building, place it in the center of the roof whenever practical. The gauge must be made as level as is possible and installed securely so that it will not be blown over.

12.5.3. Use of the Rain Gauge for Precipitation Measurements. Measure precipitation amounts collected in the rain gauge as necessary for observing and reporting requirements in **Chapter 13**, normally at 3- and 6-hourly synoptic times and at midnight LST. The gauge may be emptied more frequently if necessary for local purposes, provided a record of precipitation amounts is maintained for use in determining the total amounts for applicable 3- and 6-hourly and midnight LST observations. Obtain precipitation amounts by means of the rain gauge using the following procedures:

12.5.3.1. Measurement of Liquid Precipitation. Determine the amount of liquid precipitation amounts by measuring the collection in the rain gauge using the ML-75 measuring stick to the nearest 0.01". If only liquid precipitation has occurred during the period, the rain gauge will normally be emptied only after the 6-hourly measurement.

12.5.3.1.1. For the ML-17, slowly insert the ML-75 measuring stick into the measuring tube. Permit the stick to rest on the bottom for 2 to 3 seconds, withdraw the stick, and read the depth as the upper limit of the wet portion.

12.5.3.1.2. Whenever more than 2 inches of precipitation has fallen, the measuring tube will have overflowed, with the excess spilling into the overflow can. In such cases, obtain the total precipitation amount as follows:

12.5.3.1.2.1. Carefully remove and empty the measuring tube (when brimful, the tube contains exactly 2 inches of liquid precipitation).

12.5.3.1.2.2. Pour the liquid from the overflow container (if any) into the measuring tube and measure the amount as in **paragraph 12.5.3.1.1**

12.5.3.1.2.3. If the measuring tube is filled one or more times, record 2 inches for each instance and continue to refill the tube until the last of the overflow has been measured.

12.5.3.1.2.4. Obtain the total precipitation by adding the individual amounts measured from the overflow container and measuring tube.

12.5.3.1.2.5. When measurements have been completed, empty the measuring tube (when appropriate) and reassemble the gauge.

12.5.3.2. Measurement of Water Equivalent for Frozen/Freezing Precipitation. When frozen/freezing precipitation is expected, remove the funnel and measuring tube from the gauge and store them indoors. Determine the amount of precipitation for the observation period based on the collection in the overflow container.

12.5.3.2.1. If the collection in the overflow container is considered representative, determine the water equivalent using the following procedure:

12.5.3.2.2. Add a measured quantity of warm water to the overflow container in order to melt the contents.

12.5.3.2.3. Pour the liquid into the measuring tube, obtain a measurement, and subtract an amount equal to that of the warm water added. The result is the actual precipitation amount measured to the nearest 0.01" (e.g., the water equivalent of the frozen/freezing precipitation).

12.5.3.2.4. If the collection in the overflow can is considered unrepresentative (e.g., due to strong winds), discard the catch and obtain a measurement by means of vertical core sampling or by estimation.

12.5.3.3. Core Sampling for Water Equivalent of Frozen/Freezing Precipitation. When the collection in the rain gauge is considered unrepresentative, precipitation amounts may be determined by means of core sampling. A core sample is a section cut from the snow/ice cover at an observation location to determine the amount of water present in the solid state. Obtain the core sample in conjunction with snowfall and snow/ice depth measurements using the following procedures:

12.5.3.3.1. Invert the overflow container over the top of the snow/ice pack and lower it to the snowboard or other reference point for the new snowfall. Use the snowboard or other object to collect the sample within the area of the container.

12.5.3.3.2. Melt the collection to obtain the water content (as explained in **paragraphs 12.5.3.2.2** and **12.5.3.2.3**). Classify the amount as estimated if it is not considered representative of the actual snowfall.

Chapter 13

REPORTING AND ENCODING OF WEATHER OBSERVATIONS

13.1. Introduction. This chapter contains information on reporting and encoding weather observations.

13.2. Weather Observation METAR/SPECI Code Form. The METAR/SPECI report has two major sections: the Body (consisting of a maximum of 11 groups) and the Remarks (consisting of a maximum of 2 categories). Figure 13.1 contains the METAR/SPECI code. Table 13.1 contains the format and contents of the Body and Remarks section of a METAR/SPECI observation. Together, the body and remarks make up the complete METAR/SPECI coded report and are encoded in the order shown in **Figure 13.1**. The underline character "_" indicates a required space between the groups. The actual content of the report depends on the observation program at the individual observing organization.

Figure 13.1. Automated/Augmented METAR/SPECI Code.

METAR or SPECI	_CCCC_YYGGggZ_COR or AUTO_dddff(f)Gf$_m$f$_m$ (f$_m$)KT_d$_n$d$_n$d$_n$Vd$_x$d$_x$d$_x$_ VVVVVSM or VVVV_RD$_R$D$_R$/V$_R$V$_R$V$_R$V$_R$FT, RD$_R$D$_R$/ V$_N$V$_N$V$_N$V$_N$VV$_X$V$_X$V$_X$V$_X$FT, or RD$_R$D$_R$/V$_R$V$_R$V$_R$V$_R$, RD$_R$D$_R$/V$_N$V$_N$V$_N$V$_N$VV$_X$V$_X$V$_X$V$_X$_w'w'_N$_s$N$_s$N$_s$h$_s$h$_s$h$_s$ or VVh$_s$h$_s$h$_s$ or CLR_T'T'/T'$_d$T'$_d$_AP$_H$P$_H$P$_H$P$_H$_RMK_(Automated, Manual, Plain Language)_(Additive Data and Automated Maintenance Indicators)

Body of Report

(1) Type of Report - **METAR or SPECI**

(2) Station Identifier - **CCCC**

(3) Date and Time of Report - **YYGGggZ**

(4) Report Modifier - **COR or AUTO**

(5) Wind - **dddff(f)Gf$_m$f$_m$(f$_m$)KT_d$_n$d$_n$d$_n$Vd$_x$d$_x$d$_x$**

(6) Visibility - **VVVVVSM (or VVVV)**

(7) Runway Visual Range - **RD$_R$D$_R$/V$_R$V$_R$V$_R$V$_R$FT or RD$_R$D$_R$/V$_N$V$_N$V$_N$V$_N$VV$_X$V$_X$V$_X$V$_X$FT (or meters)**

(8) Present Weather - **w'w'**

(9) Sky Condition - **N$_s$N$_s$N$_s$h$_s$h$_s$h$_s$ or VVh$_s$h$_s$h$_s$ or CLR**

(10) Temperature and Dew Point - **T'T'/T'$_d$T'$_d$**

(11) Altimeter - **AP$_H$P$_H$P$_H$P$_H$**

Remarks Section of Report—RMK
(1) Automated, Manual and Plain Language
(2) Additive and Maintenance Data

13.3. Coding Missing Data in METAR and SPECI Reports. When an element does not occur, or cannot be observed, the corresponding group and preceding space are omitted from that particular report. When an AMOS cannot provide an element due to sensor failure, the software will automatically place a missing data flag (M) in the corresponding data field. The system will also include the maintenance indicator ($) at the end of the observation. Together, these two characters will cue the weather technicians to contact ATC agencies and maintenance and back-up the failed element.

13.4. Coding the Body of the METAR or SPECI Reports.

13.4.1. Type of Report (METAR or SPECI). The type of report, METAR or SPECI, is included in all reports. The type of report is separated from subsequent elements by a space. When SPECI criteria are met at the time of a routine report (METAR), the type of report will be a METAR.

13.4.2. Station Identifier (CCCC). The observing location identifier, CCCC, is included in all reports to identify the station generating the report. The observing location identifier consists of four alphanumeric characters if the METAR/SPECI is transmitted longline. The observing location identifier is separated from subsequent elements by a space. The agency with operational control when the location is first established is responsible for coordinating the location identifier with the FAA. A list of approved identifiers can be found in the FAA Manual 7350 Series, *Location Identifiers*. Temporary KQ-identifiers are coordinated with AFWA IAW AFMAN 15-128.

13.4.3. Date and Time of Report (YYGGggZ). The date, YY, and time, GGgg, is included in all reports. The time is the actual time the report is transmitted longline or when the criteria for a SPECI is met or noted. If the report is a correction to a previously disseminated report, the time of the corrected report will be the same time used in the report being corrected. The date and time group always ends with a "Z", indicating the use of UTC. For example, METAR KGRF 210855Z would be the 0900 scheduled report from KGRF taken at 0855 UTC on the 21st of the month.

13.4.4. Report Modifier (AUTO or COR). The report modifier can be either of the following two elements:

13.4.4.1. COR is entered into the report modifier group when a corrected METAR or SPECI is transmitted.

13.4.4.2. AUTO identifies the report as a fully automated report with no human intervention. AUTO is automatically included in reports when the weather technician signs off the ADS indicating the observations are no longer being augmented.

13.4.4.3. AUTO and COR will not be seen in the same observation. If the term COR is used, the observation cannot be reported as AUTO, since a weather technician is manually correcting the observation.

13.5. Wind Group (dddff(f)Gf$_m$f$_m$(f$_m$)KT_d$_n$d$_n$d$_n$Vd$_x$d$_x$d$_x$). The standards and procedures for observing wind are described in **Chapter 5**.

13.5.1. Direction. The true direction (ddd) the wind is blowing from is encoded in tens of degrees using three figures. Directions less than 100 degrees are preceded with a "0." For example, a wind direction of 90 is encoded "090."

13.5.2. Speed. The wind speed, ff(f), is entered as a two or three digit group immediately following the wind direction. The speed is encoded in whole knots using the tens and units digits. The hundreds digit is only used when the wind speed exceed 100 knots and is never reported as a leading zero. Speeds of less than 10 knots are encoded using a leading zero in the tens position. The group always ends with KT to indicate the wind speeds are reported in knots. For example, a wind speed of 8 knots is encoded 08KT. A wind speed of 112 knots is encoded 112KT.

13.5.3. Gust. Wind gusts are encoded in the format, Gf$_m$f$_m$(f$_m$). The wind gust is encoded in two or three digits immediately following the wind speed. The wind gust is encoded in whole knots using the units and tens digits and, if required, the hundreds digit. For example, a wind from due west at 20 knots with gusts to 35 knots would be encoded 27020G35KT.

13.5.4. Variable Wind Direction (speeds 6 knots or less). Variable wind direction with wind speed 6 knots or less may be encoded as VRB in place of the ddd. For example, if the wind is variable at three knots, it could be encoded VRB03KT.

13.5.5. Variable Wind Direction (speeds greater than 6 knots). Wind direction varying 60 degrees or more with wind speed greater than 6 knots will be encoded in the format, d$_n$d$_n$d$_n$Vd$_x$d$_x$d$_x$. The variable wind direction group will immediately follow the wind group. The directional variability will be encoded in a clockwise direction. For example, if the wind is variable from 180 to 240 at 10 knots, it would be encoded 21010KT 180V240.

13.5.6. Calm Wind. Calm wind is encoded as 00000KT.

13.6. Visibility Group (VVVVVSM). The surface visibility, VVVVVSM (VVVV in meters for OCONUS), is encoded in statute miles using the values listed in **Table 6.1** A space is encoded between whole numbers and fractions of reportable visibility values. For example, a visibility of 1 1/ 2 statute miles is encoded 1 1/2SM. The visibility group at US locations always ends in SM to indicate that visibilities are in statute miles. Only AMOS locations may use an M to indicate "less than" when reporting visibility (e.g., M1/4SM (M0400) means a visibility less than 1/4 SM as reported by AN/FMQ-19).

13.7. Runway Visual Range Group (RD$_R$D$_R$/V$_R$V$_R$V$_R$V$_R$FT). The standards and procedures for observing RVR are described in **Chapter 7**. FT at the end of the group indicates the units of measurement are in feet. Overseas locations will use measurement values as published in the DoD FLIPs (typically meters). Locations reporting in meters will not include FT or any other indicator of units.

13.7.1. RVR is encoded in the format RD$_R$D$_R$/V$_R$V$_R$V$_R$V$_R$FT, where R indicates the runway number follows, D$_R$D$_R$ is the runway number (an additional D$_R$ may be used for runway approach directions, such as R for right, L for left, and C for center), V$_R$V$_R$V$_R$V$_R$ is the constant reportable value.

13.7.2. RVR that is varying is encoded in the format, $RD_RD_R/V_NV_NV_NV_NVV_XV_XV_XV_XFT$, where R indicates the runway number follows, D_RD_R is the runway number (an additional D_R may be used for runway approach directions, such as R for right, L for left, and C for center), $V_NV_NV_NV_N$ is the lowest reportable value in feet, V separates lowest and highest visual range values, $V_XV_XV_XV_X$ is the highest reportable value. The 10-minute RVR for runway 01L varying between 1,000 and 5,000 (0300 and 1500 meters) feet would be encoded "R01L/1000V5000FT" (R01L/0300V1500).

13.7.3. If the RVR is less than its lowest reportable value, the $V_RV_RV_RV_R$ or $V_NV_NV_NV_N$ groups will be preceded by M. If the RVR is greater than its highest reportable value, the $V_RV_RV_RV_R$ or $V_XV_XV_XV_X$ groups are preceded by a P. For example, an RVR of less than 100 feet (0050 meters) will be encoded "M0100FT" (M0050); an RVR of greater than 6,000 feet (1500 meters) will be encoded "P6000FT" (P1500).

13.7.4. RVR Information Not Available (RVRNO remark). Indicates the 10-minute average touchdown RVR for the in-use runway is not available (e.g., equipment failure) during periods when prevailing visibility is 1 mile (1600 meters) or less or RVR is 6,000 feet (1830 meters) or less. RVRNO is not reported in the body of the METAR/SPECI and will be reported in the remarks IAW **Attachment 3.**

13.8. Present Weather Group (w'w'). The standards and procedures for observing present weather are described in **Chapter 8.** The following general rules apply when reporting present weather in a METAR or SPECI report:

13.8.1. Weather occurring within 5 statute miles (unless directed wlsewhere in nautical miles for thunderstorms and lightning of the point of observation (at the station) is encoded in the body of the report. Weather occurring in the vicinity of the station (between 5 and 10 statute miles unless directed elsewhere in nautical miles for thunderstorms and lightning) is also encoded in the body of the report. AMOSs will only use the vicinity (VC) qualifier with thunderstorms (TS). Augmented stations may report weather not occurring at or in the vicinity of the station in the remarks.

Table 13.1. Notations for Manually Reporting Present Weather

QUALIFIER		WEATHER PHENOMENA		
INTENSITY OR PROXIMITY 1	DESCRIPTOR 2	PRECIPITATION 3	OBSCURATION 4	OTHER 5
- Light Moderate + Heavy VC - In the Vicinity	MI shallow PR Partial BC Patches DR Low Drifting BL Blowing SH Shower(s) TS Thunderstorm FZ Freezing	DZ Drizzle RA Rain SN Snow SG Snow Grains IC Ice Crystals PL Ice Pellets GR Hail GS Small Hail and/or Snow Pellets	BR Mist FG Fog FU Smoke VA Volcanic Ash DU Widespread Dust SA Sand HZ Haze PY Spray	PO Well-Developed Dust/Sand Whirls SQ Squalls FC Funnel Cloud(s) (Tornado, or Waterspout) SS Sandstorm DS Duststorm

13.8.2. Separate groups are used for each type of present weather. Each group is separated from the other by a space. A METAR/SPECI will contain no more than three present weather groups. The groups will be ordered by priority based on Table 13.3

Table 13.2. Present Weather Reporting Order

First	- Tornadic Activity—Tornado, Funnel Cloud or Waterspout.
Second	- Thunderstorm(s) (with/without associated precipitation).
Third	- Precipitation in order of decreasing predominance—Most dominant reported first.
Fourth	- Obscurations and/or other Phenomena in order of decreasing predominance (except Tornado, Funnel Cloud or Waterspout)—Most dominant reported first.

13.8.3. The weather groups are constructed by considering columns 1 through 5 in **Table 13.2** in sequence (e.g., heavy freezing rain is encoded +FZRA).

13.8.3.1. Intensity or Proximity Qualifier.

13.8.3.1.1. Intensity Qualifier. Intensity will be encoded with all precipitation types, except ice crystals (IC), small hail and/or snow pellets (GS), and hail (GR), including those associated with a TS and those of a showery (SH) nature. No intensity will be ascribed to the obscurations of blowing dust (BLDU), blowing sand (BLSA), blowing snow (BLSN), blowing spray (BLPY), well-developed dust/sand whirls (PO) and squalls (SQ). Tornados and waterspouts are encoded as +FC, while a funnel cloud is always encoded as FC. Only moderate or heavy intensity are ascribed to sandstorm (SS) and duststorm (DS).

13.8.3.1.2. Proximity Qualifier. VC (weather phenomena observed in the vicinity of, but not at the point of observation), will only be encoded in combination with fog (FG), SH, PO, BLDU, BLSA, BLSN, SS, DS and TS. Intensity qualifiers will not be encoded with VC. VCFG will be encoded to report any type of fog in the vicinity of the point(s) of observation. Precipitation not occurring at the point of observation but within 10 statute miles will be encoded as showers in the vicinity (VCSH).

13.8.3.2. Descriptor Qualifier. Only one descriptor will be encoded for each weather phenomena group (e.g., -FZDZ). Mist (BR) will not be encoded with any descriptor.

13.8.3.2.1. The descriptors shallow (MI), partial (PR), and patches (BC) are only encoded with FG (e.g., MIFG). For MIFG (shallow fog) to be encoded, FG must cover part of the station, extend no higher than 6 feet above the ground, with visibility more than 6 feet above the ground 5/8SM (1000 meters) or more, while the apparent visibility in the FG layer is less than 5/8SM (1000 meters). For PRFG (partial fog) to be encoded, FG must cover a substantial part of the station and extend to at least 6 feet above the ground with visibility in the FG less than 5/8SM (1000 meters). For BCFG (fog patches) to be encoded, FG must randomly cover part of the station and extend to at least 6 feet above the ground with the apparent visibility in the FG patch or bank less than 5/8SM (1000 meters), while visibility over other parts of the station is greater than or equal to 5/8SM (1000 meters).

13.8.3.2.2. The descriptors low drifting (DR) and blowing (BL) is only encoded with dust (DU), sand (SA), and snow (SN) (e.g., BLSN or DRSN). DR will be encoded for DU, SA, or SN raised by the wind to less than 6 feet above the ground. When BLSN is observed with SN falling from clouds, both phenomena are reported (e.g., SN BLSN). When, because of BLSN, the weather technician cannot determine whether or not SN is also falling, then only "BLSN" will be reported. BL may also be encoded with spray (PY).

13.8.3.2.3. SH is encoded only with one or more of the precipitation types of rain (RA), SN, PL, GS or GR. The SH descriptor indicates showery-type precipitation. When showery-type precipitation is encoded with VC (VCSH), the intensity and type of precipitation is not encoded.

13.8.3.2.4. The descriptor TS may be encoded by itself, i.e., a TS without associated precipitation, or it may be encoded with the precipitation types of RA, SN, PL, GS, GR. For example, a TS with SN and GS would be encoded as "TSSNGS."

13.8.3.2.5. The descriptor freezing (FZ) is only encoded in combination with FG, drizzle (DZ) or RA (e.g., FZRA, FZFG, FZDZ).

13.8.3.3. Precipitation. AMOSs may have one type of precipitation per observation and augmented stations may have up to three types of precipitation encoded in a single present weather group. They will be encoded in decreasing predominance based on intensity. Only one intensity indicator (+ or -) may be encoded and it will refer to the first type of precipitation reported.

13.8.3.3.1. Precipitation types are DZ, RA, SN, IC, PL, GS, GR and snow grains (SG). Precipitation is reported whenever it occurs.

13.8.3.3.2. GR is reported when the diameter of the largest stones observed is 1/4 inch or more. GS is reported when the diameter of the largest hailstones is less than 1/4 inch.

13.8.3.4. Obscurations. With the exception of Volcanic Ash (VA), DRDU, DRSA, DRSN, MIFG, PRFG, and BCFG, obscurations are encoded in the body of the report if the surface visibility is less than 7 statute miles (9999 meters). Reportable obscurations are FG, Mist (BR), Smoke (FU), VA, Widespread Dust (DU), Sand (SA), Haze (HZ), and PY.

13.8.3.4.1. BR is reported when the obscuration consists of water droplets or ice crystals and the visibility is at least 5/8 SM (1000 meters), but less than 7 statute miles (9999 meters).

13.8.3.4.2. FG is reported when the obscuration consists of water droplets or ice crystals (FG or FZFG) and the visibility is less than 5/8SM (1000 meters). FZ is only reported with FG when visibility is less than 5/8 SM (1000 meters) and temperature is less than 0 degrees Celsius.

13.8.3.4.3. VA is always reported when present.

13.8.3.4.4. PY is encoded only when used with the descriptor BL.

13.8.3.5. Other Weather Phenomena.

13.8.3.5.1. SQ is reported when a sudden increase in wind speed of at least 16 knots is observed, and is sustained at 22 knots or more for at least 1 minute.

13.8.3.5.2. Funnel clouds are encoded as FC. Tornadoes or waterspouts must be encoded as +FC.

13.8.3.5.3. Sandstorms are encoded as SS, duststorms as DS. Report a moderate SS/DS when visibility is reduced to less than 5/8 statute mile (1000 meters) and greater than or equal to 5/16 statute mile (0500 meters) due to BLSA/BLDU. Report a +SS/+DS if visibility is less than 5/16 statute mile (0500 meters) due to BLSA/BLDU.

13.8.3.5.4. Well-developed sand or dust whirls are encoded as PO.

13.9. Sky Condition Group ($N_sN_sN_sh_sh_sh_s$ or $VVh_sh_sh_s$ or CLR). The standards and procedures for observing sky condition are described in **Chapter 9.**

13.9.1. Sky condition is encoded in the format, $N_sN_sN_sh_sh_sh_s$, where $N_sN_sN_s$ is the amount of sky cover and $h_sh_sh_s$ is the height of the layer. There is no space between the amount of sky cover and the height of the layer.

13.9.2. Sky condition is encoded in ascending order up to the first overcast layer. At mountain locations, if the cloud layer is below the observation location elevation, the height of the layer will be reported in the body of the METAR or SPECI as "///."

13.9.3. No more than six layers will be reported. If more than six layers are observed during back-up, weather technicians will use **Table 13.4** to help determine which layers are to be reported.

Table 13.3. Priority for Reporting Layers

Priority	Layer Description
1	Lowest few layer
2	Lowest broken layer
3	Overcast layer
4	Lowest scattered layer
5	Second lowest scattered layer
6	Second lowest broken layer
7	Highest broken layer
8	Highest scattered layer
9	Second lowest few layer
10	Highest few layer

13.9.4. Vertical visibility is encoded in the format, $VVh_sh_sh_s$, where VV identifies an indefinite ceiling and $h_sh_sh_s$ is the vertical visibility into the indefinite ceiling in hundreds of feet. There is no space between the group identifier and the vertical visibility.

13.9.5. Clear skies are encoded in the format, CLR, where CLR is the abbreviation used by all AMOS locations to indicate no clouds are present.

13.9.6. Each layer is separated from other layers by a space. The sky cover for each layer reported is encoded by using the appropriate reportable contraction from **Table 9.1** The report of clear skies (CLR) is reported by itself. The abbreviations FEW, SCT, BKN and OVC will be followed, without a space, by the height of the cloud layer.

13.9.7. The height of the base of each layer, $h_sh_sh_s$, is encoded in hundreds of feet above the surface using three digits IAW **Table 13.5**

13.9.8. A partial obscuration will be encoded with the reportable layer construction corresponding to the amount of the sky that is obscured followed by the layer height. A surface-based obscuration will have a layer height of 000. A remark will also be appended for any surface-based obscurations. For example: fog obscuring 2/8ths of the sky would be encoded in the body of the reoprt as FEW000 and clarified in the remarks as FG FEW000.

Table 13.4. Increments of Reportable Values of Sky Cover Height

Range of Height Values (feet)	Reportable Increment (feet)
5,000	To nearest 100
> 5,000 but 10,000	To nearest 500
> 10,000	To nearest 1,000

13.10. Temperature/Dew Point Group (T'T'/T'$_d$T'$_d$). The standards and procedures for observing temperature and dew point are described in **Chapter 10.**

13.10.1. The temperature is separated from the dew point following it by a solidus (/).

13.10.2. The temperature and dew point are encoded as two digits rounded to the nearest whole degree Celsius. Subzero temperatures and dew points will be prefixed with an M. For example, a temperature of 4C with a dew point of -2C is encoded as "04/M02." A temperature of -0.5C is encoded as "M00." Exception: On the electronic (Excel®) 3803, use a minus sign (-) rather than an M to indicate below zero temperature/dew points. The form macros will automatically convert the minus sign to an M on the form while retaining the numerical value of the temperature/dew point for calculations.

13.10.3. If the temperature is not available, the entire temperature/dew point group will not be encoded. If the dew point is not available, the temperature is encoded followed by a solidus (/) and no entry will be made for dew point. For example, a temperature of 1.5C and a missing dew point would be reported as "02/."

13. 11. Altimeter (AP$_H$P$_H$P$_H$P$_H$). The standards and procedures for observing altimeter are described in Chapter 11. The altimeter group always starts with an A (the international indicator for altimeter in inches of mercury). The altimeter is encoded as a four-digit group immediately following the A using the tens, units, tenths, and hundredths of inches of mercury. The decimal point is not encoded.

13.12. Remarks (RMK). Remarks generally elaborate on parameters reported in the body of the report, and will be included in all METAR and SPECI observations, if required in **Attachment 3.** Remarks will be separated from the altimeter group by a space and the contraction RMK. If there are no remarks, the contraction RMK will not be entered.

13.12.1. METAR/SPECI remarks fall into 2 major categories: (1) Automated and Augmented; and (2) Additive and Maintenance Data. **Attachment 3** gives an overview of remarks and their order of entry.

13.12.2. Remarks will be made IAW the following:

13.12.2.1. Use of Contractions and Abbreviations. Where plain language is called for, authorized contractions, abbreviations and symbols will be used to conserve time and space. However, in no case should an essential remark be omitted for the lack of readily available contractions. In such cases, the only requirement is that the remark be clear. For a detailed list of authorized contractions, see the list of abbreviations and acronyms in **Attachment 1** and FAA Order 7340 Series, *Contractions.*

13.12.2.2. Time Entries in Remarks. UTC time entries are made in minutes past the hour if the time reported occurs during the same hour the observation is taken. UTC hours and minutes are used if the hour is different from the hour of the observation or this manual prescribes the use of hour and minutes.

13.12.2.3. The reporting of Additive Data information will be IAW 24-hour UTC time for AMOS locations. If required, report snow depth during normal airfield operating hours and if a heavy snow warning is in effect. If required, report in the 0000, 0600, 1200 and 1800 UTC observation or MAJCOM specified reporting time for your installation, whenever there is more than a trace of snow on the ground and more than a a trace of precipitation (water equivalent) has occurred within the past 6 hours.

13.12.2.4. Location Entries. Phenomena encoded in the body of the report as vicinity (VC) may be further described, (e.g., direction from the observing location, if known). Phenomena beyond 10 statute miles of the point of observation may be reported as distant (DSNT) if the actual distance is unknown but believed to be beyond 10 statute miles, followed by the direction from the observing location. If known, the distance in statute miles (CONUS) or meters (OCONUS) may be included in the remark. In the case of a tornado, the exact location should be included, if possible.

13.12.2.5. Movement Entries. Movement of clouds or weather, if known, will be encoded with respect towards the direction the phenomenon is moving. For example, a thunderstorm 9 statute miles north moving toward the northeast would be encoded as "TS 9N MOV NE."

13.12.2.6. Direction. Directions will use the eight points of the compass encoded in a clockwise order beginning with north. In the event that the reported phenomena is north but also extends northwest and northeast, record the phenomena in a clockwise direction (e.g., TS 10NW-NE).

13.13. Dissemination. All observations will be disseminated local and longline in the METAR/SPECI code format. Most EUs will use an ADS as the primary local and longline dissemination system. During periods when the ADS system is unavailable, EUs should use AFW-WEBS, the Secure Joint Air Force and Army Weather Information Network (JAAWIN-S), OWS or another EU to disseminate observations longline. **Figure 13.2** contains example METAR/SPECI augmented observations.

13.13.1. **Pressure altitude (PA) and density altitude (DA) are normally only disseminated locally.** When required, disseminate PA (e.g., PA +130) or DA (e.g., DA +3680) following the last element or remark in the observation, with the exception of runway condition remarks which are reported last.

13.13.2. As capability exists, EU will configure ADS systems to provide an **URGENT** alert to users on the local weather dissemination network upon receipt of reports for Tornadic Activity and Volcanic Eruptions, and for other reports of severe weather that could cause an immediate threat to life or property.

13.13.3. Corrections (COR) to Transmitted Data. When correcting observations, the COR will be disseminated in the same manner as the observation being corrected. Disseminate CORs as soon as possible whenever an error is detected in a transmitted report. However, if the erroneous data has been corrected or superseded by a later report (with the same or more complete dissemination), do not transmit the corrected observation. Transmitted corrections will consist of the entire corrected observation. Use the original date and time of the observation as the date and time in the COR'd observation, along with a remark containing the UTC time of transmission. See **Attachment 3**.

Figure 13.2. Examples of Augmented Longline Dissemination of METARs/SPECIs

Augmented METAR Observations
METAR ETAR 010756Z VRB06KT 1400 R09/1220 -RA BR FEW000 SCT008 OVC012 01/M01 A2938 RMK AO2A TWR VIS 1600 VIS N 3200 CIG 010V015 BR FEW000 SLPNO ALSTG ESTMD;
METAR KSTV 011058Z COR 02010G17KT 1400 R36/4000 HZ SCT007 BKN020 OVC070 20/17 A3019 RMK AO2A SLP015 ALSTG/SLP ESTMD COR 1104;
METAR KHLN 011158Z 27004KT 3/4SM R32/P6000FT -RA BR FEW000 SCT005 OVC020 00/M01 A2992 RMK AO2A TWR VIS 2 BR FEW000 SLP982 ALSTG/SLP ESTMD 60010 70100 4/002 10010 21002 52010;
METAR EOIN 011157Z 30003KT 9999 CLR M04/M10 A3003 RMK AO2A SLP985 70010 4/002;
METAR RKTG 010358Z 00000KT 0800 FG VV011 24/24 A2998 RMK AO2A TWR VIS 1000 SLP982 RVRNO;
METAR ETAB 010655Z 24010G18KT 9999 TS SCT020CB BKN035 30/27 A2993 RMK AO2A TS 4SW MOV NE SLPNO;
METAR KGRF 011157Z 24012KT 10SM -TSRA FEW008 FEW025TCU SCT030CB 25/17 A2992 RMK AO2A PK WND 28045/10 TS 2NE MOV SE FU FEW008 SCT030 V BKN TCU SE-S SLPNO 60010 70010 52010;

Augmented SPECI Observations
SPECI ETAR 010731Z 25003KT 1600 BR BKN006 10/06 A3002 RMK AO2A CIG 004V008 RVRNO;
SPECI RJFA 011614Z 02005KT 0600 R36/2400 -DZ FG SCT000 SCT006 SCT016 02/M03 A2981 RMK AO2A TWR VIS 1000 VIS 0400V0800 FG SCT000;
SPECI KFAW 010812Z 24020G40KT 1 1/2SM +FC +TSRAGR SQ FEW030CB SCT040 BKN050 25/22 A2992 RMK TORNADO 3SW MOV NE FUNNEL CLOUD B02E09 3W MOV NE AO2A TWR VIS 2 1/2 VIS SW 2 TSB59 TS 5S-3W MOV NE GR 1/2 PRESFR;

13.13.4. Local Dissemination. During ADS outages or if ADS is not available, disseminate observations first to ATC. For further dissemination, establish procedures locally in an order of priority that is consistent with local requirements and scheduled file times for longline transmission. Coordinate local dissemination procedures to include code form, format and content with local customers and document in the local weather documentation. Locations without an ADS should disseminate observations locally as follows:

13.13.4.1. Precede reports of tornadic activity, volcanic eruptions and other reports of severe weather that could cause an immediate threat to life or property, with the term **URGENT**.

13.13.4.2. Disseminate wind direction in degrees <u>magnetic</u> (unless otherwise specificed, see **Chapter 5**) using three digits.

13.13.4.3. Disseminate all other plain language remarks as required by local agencies after the last element of the observation.

13.13.4.4. Maintain a copy of all observations disseminated locally.

13.13.5. Voice Dissemination. Maintain instructions outlining priorities and procedures to follow for local dissemination of observations by voice relay (e.g., read back by the person receiving the data). Disseminate all observations immediately to local ATC agencies (e.g., tower, Radar Approach Control, Ground Control Approach), then to other users as established locally. Also maintain a record (written or recording) of all the following when voice is used to disseminate locally during outages of the primary system:

13.13.5.1. Actual time of observation (UTC).

13.13.5.2. Time (in minutes past the hour) the observation was transmitted to the tower and other local ATC agencies.

13.13.5.3. Single element LOCALs for Altimeter setting, PA or DA (where required).

13.13.5.4. Initials of the weather technician making the dissemination and the initials of the receiver at the supported agency.

13.13.6. Supplementary Identification of Observations. At limited-duty EUs and gunnery ranges, identify the last observation of the day (METAR or SPECI) by adding the term "LAST" following the last element in the observation text (e.g., TCU SE LAST), and include the remark on the 3803/3813, as applicable.

13.13.7. Delayed Reports. Transmit the contraction NIL at the standard time when it is evident that a weather report will not be completed in time for scheduled transmission.

13.13.8. Reports Filed But not Transmitted. When an augmented observation is not able to be transmitted longline before the next METAR or SPECI is required, transmit only the latest observation longline. Enter "FIBI" (contraction for *Filed But Impractical to Transmit*) in parenthesis in column 13 (FIBI). Include FIBI in a METAR only if a later observation containing all elements of a METAR is available for transmission.

13.13.9. When a SPECI is not transmitted longline, transmit subsequent SPECI only when the change between the last transmitted report and the current report meets the criteria for a SPECI. Otherwise, enter (FIBI) in remarks for the current report and only disseminate it locally.

13.14. Reports of a Volcanic Eruption. Reports of a Volcanic Eruption are disseminated regardless of the delay. Use any reasonable means to disseminate the report.

13.15. Communication Failure. If all longline communication services have failed (e.g., ADS and no Internet connection), telephone the METAR or SPECI during the failure to the nearest OWS or EU with communication capability.

13.16. Longline Dissemination by other EUs. Enter a record of longline dissemination by another EU in parentheses in column 13 of AF 3803/3813. Identify the EU that transmitted the observation longline and the initials of the individual that received the data (e.g., (BY KGRF/DR), (BY 25 OWS/MS)).

13.17. Quality Control of Observations. EUs will establish procedures to check all manually entered surface weather observations for erroneous data before dissemination and again after dissemination before the next observation to verify that no errors were generated during the dissemination process.

BURTON M. FIELD, Lt Gen, USAF
DSC/Operations, Plans & Requirements

Attachment 1

GLOSSARY OF REFERENCES AND SUPPORTING INFORMATION

References

DoD 8570.01-M, *Information Assurance Workforce Improvement Program,* 24 January, 2012

DoD Flight Information Publications (FLIPS)

AFDD 1, *Air Force Basic Doctrine, Organization, and Command,* 14 October 2011

AFPD 15-1, *Air Force Weather Operations,* 19 February 2010

AFI 10-229, *Responding to Severe Weather Events*, 15 October 2003

AFI 11-201, *Flight Information Publication,* 31 March 2009

AFI 13-204, Volume 3, *Airfield Operations Procedures and Programs*, 1 September 2010

AFI 15-127, *Air Force Weather Qualification Training*, 14 March 2012

AFI 15-128, *Air Force Weather Roles and Responsibilities,* 7 February 2011

AFMAN 15-129, Volume 2, *Air and Space Weather Operations – Exploitation*, 7 December 2011

FAAO JO 7340.2, *Federal Aviation Administration Handbook, Contractions,* 9 February, 2012

FAAO JO 7350.8D, *Federal Aviation Administration Handbook, Location Identifiers,* 5 June 2008

FAAO JO 7110.65, *Air Traffic Control,* 9 February 2012

Federal Meteorological Handbook No. 1 (FCM-H1), *Surface Weather Observations and Reports,* September 2005

FCM-S4-1994, *Federal Standard for Siting Meteorological Sensors at Airports*, August 1994

World Meteorological Organization, WMO-No. 306, Manual on Codes, Vol I, *International Codes,* 2011 Edition

WMO-No. 306, Manual on Codes, Vol II, *Regional Codes and National Coding Practices,* 2011 Edition

Presribed Forms

AF 3803 – *Surface Weather Observations (METAR/SPECI)*, 01 August 2000

Adopted Forms

AF 847 – *Recommendation for Change of Publication,* 22 September 2009

AF 3622 – *Air Traffic Control/Weather Certification and Rating Record (LRA),* 1 June 1991

Abbreviations and Acronyms

- - Light intensity

no symbol— - Moderate intensity

+ -Heavy intensity

/ - Indicates visual range data follows; separator between temperature and dew point data.

ACC—Altocumulus Castellanus

ACFT MSHP—Aircraft Mishap

ACSL—Altocumulus Standing Lenticular Cloud

ADS—Automated Dissemination System

AFWA—Air Force Weather Agency

AFW—WEBS – Air Force Weather Web Servcies

ALSTG—Altimeter Setting

AMOS—Automatic Meteorological Observing System

AO1—ASOS/AWOS stations without a precipitation discriminator

AO2—Remark included in METAR/SPECI observations from AN/FMQ-19 EUs without augmentation (or ASOS/AWOS stations with a precipitation discriminator)

AO2A—Remark included in METAR/SPECI observations from AN/FMQ-19 EUs with manual augmentation

AOL—Alternate Operating Location

APRNT—Apparent

APRX—Approximately

ASOS—Automated Surface Observing System

ATC—Air Traffic Control

ATIS—Automatic Terminal Information Service

AURBO—Aurora

AUTO—Automated Report

AWIPS—Advanced Weather Interactive Processing System

B——Began

BC—Patches

BKN—Broken

BL—Blowing

BR—Mist

BWW—Basic Weather Watch

C——Center (With Reference To Runway Designation)

CB—Cumulonimbus Cloud

CBMAM—Cumulonimbus Mammatus Cloud

CCSL—Cirrocumulus Standing Lenticular Cloud

CHI—Cloud-Height Indicator

CHINO LOC—Cloud-height-indicator, Sky Condition At Secondary Location Not Available

CIG—Ceiling

CLR—Clear

CONS—Continuous

CONTRAILS—Condensation Trails

CONUS—Continental United States

COR—Correction to A Previously Disseminated Report

CWW—Continuous Weather Watch

DOD—Department Of Defense

DR—Low Drifting

DS—Duststorm

DSNT—Distant

DU—Widespread Dust

DZ—Drizzle

E— —East, Ended

ESTMD—Estimated

FAA—Federal Aviation Administration

FC—Funnel Cloud

FCM—H1 —Federal Meteorological Handbook No. 1, Surface Weather Observations & Reports

FEW—Few Clouds

FG—Fog

FIBI—Filed But Impracticable To Transmit

FIRST—First Observation After A Break In Coverage At An Augmented Observing EU

FLIP—Flight Information Publication

FROPA—Frontal Passage

FRQ—Frequent

FT—Feet

FU—Smoke

FZ—Freezing

FZRANO—Freezing Rain Information Not Available

G— —Gust

GEN—Indicates General Aeronautical Contraction Usage

GR—Hail

GS—Small Hail and/or Snow Pellets

HPa— —Hectopascals (millibars)

HZ—Haze

IAW—In Accordance With

IC—Ice Crystals

ICAO—International Civil Aviation Organization

IFR—Instrument Flight Rules

ILS—Instrument Landing System

JAAWIN—S —Secure Joint Air Force and Army Weather Information Network

JET—Joint Environmental Toolkit

KT—Knots

L——Left (With Reference To Runway Designation)

LAST—Last Observation Before A Break In Coverage At An Augmented Observing EU

LBC—Laser-Beam Ceilometer

LST—Local Standard Time

LTG—Lightning

LWR—Lower

M— —Minus, Less Than

MAJCOM—Major Air Force Command

METAR—Aviation Routine Weather Report

MI—Shallow

MMLS—Mobil Microwave Landing System

MOV—Move, Moving, Moved

MT—Mountains

N— —North

N/A—Not Applicable

NE—Northeast

NW—Northwest

NWS—National Weather Service

OCNL—Occasional

OCONUS—Outside Continental United States

OFCM—Office of the Federal Coordinator for Meteorology

OHD—Overhead

OVC—Overcast

P— —Greater Than (used with RVR)

PAR—Precision Approach Radar

PCPN—Precipitation

PK WND—Peak Wind

PL—Ice Pellets

PNO—Precipitation Amount Not Available

PO—Dust/Sand Whirls (Dust Devils)

PR—Partial

PRESFR—Pressure Falling Rapidly

PRESRR—Pressure Rising Rapidly

PV—Prevailing Visibility

PWINO—Precipitation Identifier Sensor Not Available

PY—Spray

R— —Right (With Reference To Runway Designation)

RA—Rain

RMK—Remark

RVR—Runway Visual Range

RVRNO—Runway Visual Range Information Not Available

RWY—Runway

S——South

SA—Sand

SCSL—Stratocumulus Standing Lenticular Cloud

SCT—Scattered

SE—Southeast

SFC—Surface

SG—Snow Grains

SH—Shower(s)

SLP—Sea Level Pressure

SLPNO—Sea Level Pressure Not Available

SM—Statute Miles

SN—Snow

SNINCR—Snow Increasing Rapidly

SPECI—Aviation Selected Special Weather Report (An unscheduled report taken when certain criteria have been met)

SQ—Squall

SS—Sandstorm

SW—Southwest

TCU—Towering Cumulus

TS—Thunderstorm

TSNO—Thunderstorm Information Not Available

TWR—Tower

UNKN—Unknown

UP—Unknown Precipitation

UTC—Coordinated Universal Time

V——Variable

VA—Volcanic Ash

VC—In the Vicinity

VFR—Visual Flight Rules

VIS—Visibility

VISNO LOC—Visibility at Secondary Location Not Available

VRB—Variable

VV—Vertical Visibility

W——West

WMO—World Meteorological Organization

WND—Wind

WSHFT—Wind Shift

Z——Zulu (e.g., Coordinated Universal Time)

Terms

At the Station—Used to report present weather phenomena when within 5 statute miles/8000 meters of the point(s) of observation.

Aviation Routine Weather Report—The WMO METAR code format used worldwide to encode weather observations.

Distant from the Station—Used to report present weather phenomena more than 10 statute miles/16 kilometers from the point(s) of observation.

Eyes Forward—EU technicians are the eyes forward for the OWS forecasters and integrate weather radar data, meteorological satellite imagery, lightning detection readouts, and non-standard weather data systems (vertical profilers, mesonet data, etc.) to create an integrated weather picture and near-term trend forecasts for the OWS. Eyes forward yields meaningful meteorological information not contained in coded observations to the servicing OWS and is an integral part of the meteorological watch for an installation or contingency operating location.

File Time—The specific time or specific time block a weather message or bulletin is scheduled to be transmitted.

Freezing Rain—Rain that falls in liquid form but freezes upon impact to form a coating of glaze upon the ground and on exposed objects. While the temperature of the ground surface and glazed objects initially must be near or below freezing, it is necessary that the water drops be supercooled before striking (AMS, Glossary of Meteorology, 1989).

Glaze—A coating of ice, generally clear and smooth but usually containing some air pockets, formed on exposed objects by the freezing of a film of supercooled water deposited by rain, drizzle, fog, or possible condensed from supercooled water vapor. Glaze is denser, harder and more transparent then either rime or hoarfrost. Its density may be as high as 0.8 or 0.9 gm per cm3. Factors that favor glaze formation are large drop size, rapid accretion, slight supercooling, and slow dissipation of heat fusion (AMS, Glossary of Meteorology, 1989).

ICAO Identifier—A specifically authorized 4-letter identifier assigned to a location and documented in ICAO Document 7910.ICAO.

International Civil Aviation Organization—A United Nations organization specializing in matters dealing with international aviation and navigation.

Joint Environmental Toolkit (JET)—JET consolidates and integrates key capabilities from several familiar systems (N-TFS, OPS-II, JWIS, AOS, IWWC, IWEDA, IMETS…) used in OWSs, EUs, AOCs, and even deployed into one seamless application.

Limited—Duty Exploitation Unit—A EU that provides less than 24-hour a day forecast service.

Notice to Airmen (NOTAM)—A timely notice containing information concerning the establishment, condition, or change in any aeronautical facility, service, procedures, or hazards, essential to personnel concerned with flight operations.

Observed—Indicates reported weather information was determined visually by weather personnel, or weather sensing equipment, or by using radar.

Pilot Report (PIREP)—A report of in-flight weather provided by an aircraft crewmember.

Severe Weather—Any weather condition that poses a hazard to property or life.

Vicinity—Used to report present weather phenomena 5 statute miles/8000 meters to 10 statute miles/16 kilometers from the point(s) of observation.

Attachment 2

SPECIAL (SPECI) CRITERIA

Table A2.1. Table of SPECI Criteria

Number	Reference	Criteria	Pertinent data	Manual	Automated	Supplement	Back-up
1		**Visibility** (1) 3 statute miles/4800 meters (See Notes 1 & 2). (2) 2 statute miles/3200 meters (See Note 3). (3) 1 mile/1600 meters (See Note 4). (4) ¼ mile/400 meters (if a blizzard warning is required for the location). (5) All published airfield landing minima (including circling), as listed in the DoD FLIPs, appropriate Air Force, Army, HQ, or MAJCOM instructions and publications. If none is published, use 1/2 mile/800 meters (See Notes 5 & 7). (6) Visibility minima as applicable to range support, covered in governing directives and support agreements. (7) All published airfield takeoff minima	Surface visibility as reported in the body of the report decreases to less than or, if below, increases to equal or exceed.	X	X	X(*)	X

Number	Reference	Criteria	Pertinent data	Manual	Automated	Supplement	Back-up
2		**Ceiling** (1) 3,000 feet (See Note 1). (2) 2,000 feet (See Note 2) (3) 1,500 feet (See Note 2). (4) 1,000 feet (See Note 3). (5) 800 feet (See Note 4). (6) 700 feet (See Note 5). (7) 500 feet (See Note 6). (8) 300 feet (See Note 7). (9) All published airfield landing minima (including circling), as listed in DoD FLIPs and appropriate USAF, Army, HQ, or MAJCOM flying instructions and publications. If none published, use 200 feet (See Note 7). (10) Ceiling minima, as applicable to range support, covered in governing directives and support agreements. (11) All published airfield takeoff minima	The ceiling (rounded off to reportable values) forms or dissipates below, decreases to less than, or if below, increases to equal or exceed.	X	X	O	X
3		**Sky Condition**	A layer of clouds or obscuring phenomena aloft is observed below the highest published instrument landing minimum (including circling) applicable to the airfield, and no layer aloft was reported below this height in the previous	X	X	O	X

		METAR or SPECI.				
4	**Wind Shift**	Wind direction changes by 45 degrees or more in less than 15 minutes and the wind speed is 10 knots or more throughout the wind shift.	X	X	O	X
5	**Squall**	When squalls occur.	X	X	O	X

Number	Reference	Criteria	Pertinent data	Manual	Automated	Supplement	Back-up
6		**Volcanic Eruption** (See Remark 1, **Table A3.1.**)	Eruption or volcanic ash cloud first noted.	X	O	X	O
7		**Thunderstorm** (occurring at the station) (1) Begins. (2) Ends.	A SPECI is not required to report the beginning of a new thunderstorm if one is currently reported.	X	X	O	X
8		**Precipitation** (1) Hail begins or ends. (2) Freezing precipitation begins, ends, or changes intensity. (3) Ice pellets begin, end, or change intensity. (4) Any other type of precipitation begins or ends (N/A for ASOS).	**Note:** Except for freezing rain, freezing drizzle, hail, and ice pellets, a SPECI is not required for changes in type (e.g., drizzle changing to snow grains) or the beginning or ending of one type while another is in progress (e.g., snow changing to rain and snow).	X(*) X X X	O X O X	X(*) O X O	O X O X
9		**Tornado, Funnel Cloud, or Waterspout** (1) Is observed. (2) Disappears from sight or ends.		X	O	X	O

Number	Reference	Criteria	Pertinent data	Manual	Automated	Supplement	Back-up
10		**Runway Visual Range (RVR)** (1) Prevailing visibility first observed ≤ 1SM/1600 meters, again when prevailing visibility goes above 1SM/1600 meters. (2) RVR for active runway decrease to less than or, if below, increase to equal or exceed: (a) 6,000 feet (P1500 meters for AMOS sensors, 1830 meters for ASOS sensors) (b) 5,000 feet (1500 meters for AMOS sensors, 1520 meters for ASOS sensors) (c) 2400 feet (0750 meters for AMOS sensors, 0730 meters for ASOS sensors) (d) 2,000 feet (0600 meters for AMOS sensors, 0610 meters for ASOS sensors) Required for CAT I and II ILS Localizer Critical Areas, Precision Approach Radar (PAR) Touchdown Areas, and MMLS Azimuth Critical Area. (3) All published RVR minima applicable to the runway in use. (4) RVR is first determined as unavailable (RVRNO) for the runway is use, and when it is first determined that the RVRNO report is no longer applicable, provided conditions for reporting RVR exist.	The highest value during the preceding 10 minutes from the designated RVR runway decreases to less than, or if below, increases to equal or exceed. **Note:** The RVR SPECI observations will be taken, but will only be transmitted longline by EUs with a 10-minute RVR average readout capability.	X	X	O	X

Reference	Criteria	Pertinent data	Manual	Automated	Supplement	Back-up
11	**Upon Resumption of Observing Function**	A special (SPECI) observation will be taken within 15-minutes after the weather technician returns to duty following a break in observing coverage or augmentation at the observing location unless a METAR observation is filed during that 15-minute period	X	O	X	X
12	**Criteria Established Locally.** EUs will take a SPECI for any criteria significant to local installation operations (e.g., alert observations). These criteria will be coordinated with base agencies and specified in the base/host unit's plans or weather support document.		X	X	O	X
14	**Miscellaneous**	Any other meteorological situation that, in the weather technician's opinion, is critical	O	O	O	O

NOTES:

X - Indicates required data

O - Indicates optional data based on local operational requirements

1. Fixed-Wing Alternate Requirement, AFI 11-202V3.

2. Fixed-Wing IFR, AFI 11-202V3.

3. Qualified Fixed-Wing Alternate, AFI 11-202V3.

4. Required for CAT I and II Instrument Landing System (ILS) Localizer Critical Areas, CAT I and II ILS Glide Slope Critical Areas, Mobil Microwave Landing System (MMLS) Azimuth Critical Area, and MMLS Elevation Critical Area.

NOTES (cont):

5. Qualified Helicopter Alternate, AFI 11-202V3, AR 95-1, OPNAVINST 3710.7.

6. Helicopter IFR, AFI 11-202V3, AR 95-1, OPNAVINST 3710.7.

7. At bases with assigned Air Defense Aircraft, USAF NR-15-1 (NORAD).

8. A SPECI observation is not required for in-flight emergencies, i.e., those declared to reflect an unsafe condition that could adversely affect the safety of the aircraft. However, such in-flight emergencies should alert weather personnel to intensify the weather watch to ensure maximum support to the aircraft in distress. If the in-flight emergency results in an accident or incident, the aircraft mishap SPECI is then required.

Note: If in doubt, take the observation.

* - See Table 3.1

Attachment 3

REMARKS

Table A3.1. Automated, Manual, and Plain Language Remarks/Additive and Maintenance Data

Remark Number	Observed Condition	Enter in Remarks Section	Manual	Automated	Supplement	Back-up
1	Volcanic Eruption	Report the following information, if known: (1) Name of volcano, (2) Latitude and longitude or direction and distance from the EU, (3) Date/time UTC of eruption, (4) Size description, approximate height and direction of movement of the ash cloud, (5) And any other pertinent data, e.g., MT AUGUSTINE VOLCANO 70 STATUTE MILES SW ERUPTED 231505 LARGE ASH CLOUD EXTENDING TO APRX 30000 FT MOV NE.	X		X	X
2	Tornadic Activity (See Note1)	Encode tornadoes, funnel clouds, or waterspouts in format, **Tornadic activity_B/E(hh)mm_ LOC/DIR_(MOV)**, where TORNADO, FUNNEL CLOUD, or WATERSPOUT identifies the specific tornadic activity, B/E denotes the beginning and/or ending time, (hh)mm is the time of occurrence (only the minutes are required if the hour can be inferred from the report time), LOC/DIR is the location (distance if known) and/or direction of the phenomena from the EU, and MOV is the movement, if known. Tornadic activity will be encoded as the first remark after the "RMK" entry. For example, "TORNADO B13 6 NE" would indicate that a tornado, which began at 13 minutes past the hour, was 6 statute miles northeast of the observing location.	X		X	X
3	Augmented or Automated Systems	**(AO2 or AO2A).** Encode **AO2** in all METAR/SPECI from AMOSs without augmentation. Encode **AO2A** in all METAR/SPECI from AMOSs with manual augmentation. **Note:** ASOS/AWOS stations without a precipitation discriminator will report AO1; ASOS/AWOS stations with a precipitation discriminator will report AO2.		X	X	X

Remark Number	Observed Condition	Enter in Remarks Section	Manual	Automated	Supplement	Back-up
4	Peak Wind	Encode peak wind (> 25 knots) in format, **PK_WND_dddff(f)/(hh)mm** (FMQ-19 will encode time in an HHMM format) of the next METAR, where PK_WND is the remark identifier, ddd is the direction of the peak wind, ff(f) is the peak wind speed since the last METAR, and (hh)mm is the time of occurrence (only the minutes are required if the hour can be inferred from the report time). There will be a space between the two elements of the remark identifier and the wind direction/speed group; a solidus "/" (without spaces) will separate the wind direction/speed group and the time. This remark is still required even if the peak wind speed was transmitted in an intervening SPECI, but is not required if the peak wind occurred and/or reoccurred during the 2-minute observation period prior to the METAR. For example, a peak wind of 45 knots from 280 degrees that occurred at 15 minutes past the hour would be encoded "PK WND 28045/15." Multiple occurrence example: PK WND 24042/43 25042/19 (augmented EUs). **Note**: AN/FMQ-19 reports the most recent occurrence of the peak wind.	X	X		X
5	Wind Shift	Encode wind shift ($\geq 45°$ in less than 15 minutes with sustained winds ≥ 10 kts) in format, **WSHFT_(hh)mm** (FMQ-19 will encode time in an HHMM format), where WSHFT is the remark identifier and (hh)mm is the time the wind shift began. When augmenting, the contraction **FROPA** may be manually entered by the weather technician following the time if it is reasonably certain that the wind shift was the result of a frontal passage. There is a space between the remark identifier and the time and, if applicable, between the time and the frontal passage contraction. For example, a remark reporting a wind shift accompanied by a frontal passage that began at 30 minutes after the hour would be encoded as "WSHFT 30 FROPA."	X	X		X

Remark Number	Observed Condition	Enter in Remarks Section	Manual	Automated	Supplement	Back-up
6	Tower or Surface Visibility	Encode tower visibility as, **TWR_VIS_vvvvv** where vvvvv is the observed tower visibility value when surface and/or tower visibility are less than 4 statute miles (6000 meters) and differ by a reportable value from the surface visibility. There is a space between each of the remark elements. For example, the surface visibility is 1 statute mile (1600 meters) and tower visibility is 1 1/2 statute miles (2400 meters) you would encode TWR VIS 1 1/2 (TWR VIS 2400).	O			
7	Variable Prevailing Visibility	Encode variable prevailing visibility (visibility < 3 statute miles (4800 meters) increases/decreases by 1/2 SM (0800 meters) during observation) in format $VIS\_v_nv_nv_nv_nv_nVv_xv_xv_xv_xv_x$, where VIS is the remark identifier, $v_nv_nv_nv_nv_n$ is the lowest visibility evaluated, V denotes variability between two values, and $v_xv_xv_xv_xv_x$ is the highest visibility evaluated. There is one space following the remark identifier; no spaces between the letter V and the lowest/highest values. For example, a visibility that was varying between 1/2 and 2 statute miles would be encoded "VIS 1/2V2."	X	X		X
8	Sector Visibility	Encode sector visibility (visibility in ≥ 45° sector differs from prevailing visibility by one or more reportable values and either prevailing or sector visibility is < 3 statute miles (4800 meters) in format, **VIS_[DIR]_vvvvv_[Plain Language],** where VIS is the remark identifier, [DIR] defines the sector to 8 points of the compass, and vvvvv is the sector visibility in statute miles or meters, using the appropriate set of values. For example, a visibility of 2 1/2 statute miles (4000 meters) in the northeastern octant would be encoded "VIS NE 2 1/2" (VIS NE 4000).	O			
9	Visibility At Second Location	Encode visibility at a second location in format **VIS_vvvvv_[LOC],** where VIS is the remark identifier, vvvvv is the measured visibility value, and [LOC] is the specific location of the visibility sensor(s) at the EU. Include the remark only when the condition is lower than that contained in the body of the report. For example, a visibility of 2 1/2 statute miles (4000 meters) measured by a second sensor located at runway 11 would be encoded "VIS 2 1/2 RWY11" (VIS 4000 RWY11).		X		

Remark Number	Observed Condition	Enter in Remarks Section	Manual	Automated	Supplement	Back-up
10	Lightning	**Automated (including Augmented) Observing Locations.** When lightning is detected: – Within 5 nautical miles of the detector, it will report **TS** in the body of the report with no remark; – Between 5 and 10 nautical miles of the detector, it will report **VCTS** in the body of the report with no remark; – Beyond 10 but less than 30 nautical miles of the detector, report it as LTG DSNT followed by the direction from the sensor (e.g., **LTG DSNT W).**	X	X		X
11	**Beginning and Ending of Precipitation**	Encode beginning and ending of precipitation in format, **w'w'B(hh)mmE(hh)mm** (FMQ-19 will encode on all observations up to and including the next METAR with time encoded in an HHMM format), where w'w' is the type of precipitation, B denotes the beginning, E denotes the ending, and (hh)mm is the time of occurrence (only the minutes are required if the hour can be inferred from the report time). There are no spaces between the elements. The encoded remarks are not required in SPECI and should be reported in the next METAR. Do not encode intensity qualifiers. For example, if rain began at 0005, ended at 0030, and snow began at 0020, and ended at 0055, the remarks would be encoded "RAB05E30SNB20E55." If the precipitation were showery, the remark would be encoded "SHRAB05E30SHSNB20E55."		X		O

Remark Number	Observed Condition	Enter in Remarks Section	Manual	Automated	Supplement	Back-up
12	**Beginning and Ending of Thunderstorms** (See Note 1)	Encode beginning and ending of thunderstorm(s) in format, **TSB(hh)mmE(hh)mm**, where TS indicates thunderstorm, B denotes the beginning, E denotes the ending, and (hh)mm is the time of occurrence (only the minutes are required if the hour can be inferred from the report time). There are no spaces between the elements. For example, if a thunderstorm began at 0159 and ended at 0230, the remark would be encoded "TSB0159E30." AMOSs automatically provide a remark both when the thunderstorm begins and ends (e.g., TSB1635 indicates a thunderstorm began at 1635Z).	X	X		X
13	**Thunderstorm Location**	Encode thunderstorm(s) in format, **TS_LOC_(MOV_DIR)**, where TS identifies the thunderstorm activity, LOC is the location (distance if known) of the thunderstorm(s) from the EU, and MOV_DIR is the movement with direction, if known. For example, a thunderstorm 8 statute miles southeast of the EU and moving toward the northeast would be encoded "TS 8SE MOV NE."	O			
14	**Hailstone Size**	Encode Hailstone size $\geq$ local warning criteria in format, **GR_[size]_[Plain Language]**, where GR is the remark identifier and [size] is the diameter of the largest hailstone. The hailstone size is encoded in 1/4 inch increments. For example, "GR 1 3/4" would indicate that the largest hailstones were 1 3/4 inches in diameter. If **GS** is encoded in the body of the report, no hailstone size remark is required.	X(*)		X(*)	X(*)
15	**Variable Ceiling Height**	Encode variable ceiling height (height variable and ceiling layer below 3000 feet) in format, **CIG_$h_n h_n h_n$V$h_x h_x h_x$**, where CIG is the remark identifier, hnhnhn is the lowest ceiling height evaluated, V denotes variability between two values, and hxhxhx is the highest ceiling height evaluated. There is one space following the remark identifier; no spaces between the letter V and the lowest/highest ceiling values. For example, "CIG 005V010" would indicate a ceiling that was varying between 500 and 1,000 feet.	X	X		X

Remark Number	Observed Condition	Enter in Remarks Section	Manual	Automated	Supplement	Back-up
16	Partial Obscurations	Encode partial obscurations (surface-based or aloft) in format, **w'w'_[$N_sN_sN_s$]$h_sh_sh_s$_[Plain Language]**, where w'w' is the present weather causing the obscuration at the surface or aloft, and $N_sN_sN_s$ is the applicable sky cover amount of the obscuration aloft (FEW, SCT, BKN, OVC) or at the surface (FEW, SCT, BKN), and $h_sh_sh_s$ is the applicable height. Surface-based obscurations will have a height of "000." There is a space separating the weather causing the obscuration and the sky cover amount, and no space between the sky cover amount and the height. For example, fog hiding 3-4 oktas of the sky would be encoded "FG SCT000." A broken layer of smoke at 2,000 feet would be encoded "FU BKN020."	O			
17	Variable Sky Condition	Encode variable sky condition (sky condition below 3,000 feet that varies between one or more reportable values (FEW, SCT, BKN, OVC) during the period of observation) in format, **$N_sN_sN_s$($h_sh_sh_s$)_V_$N_sN_sN_s$_[Plain Language]**, where $N_sN_sN_s$($h_sh_sh_s$) is the predominant sky condition $N_sN_sN_s$ is the varying sky condition, and V denotes the variability between the two ranges. For example, SCT V BKN" would identify a scattered layer that is variably broken. If there are several layers with the same sky condition amount in the report, the layer height will be coded with the variable layer. For example, an observation with cloud layers of SCT010 BKN014 BKN020 with a cloud layer at 1,400 feet that is varying between broken and overcast would be coded "BKN014 V OVC."	X	X		X

Remark Number	Observed Condition	Enter in Remarks Section	Manual	Automated	Supplement	Back-up
18	**Significant Cloud Types**	Encode significant cloud types as follows. Identify cumulonimbus (CB) of any kind and towering cumulus (TCU) in the body of the report in the sky condition group. Include distance if known. (1) **Cumulonimbus or Cumulonimbus Mammatus** as appropriate, (when no thunderstorm is being reported) in format **(CB or CBMAM_LOC_(MOV_DIR)_[Plain Language]** where CB or CBMAM is the cloud type, LOC is the direction from the observing location, and MOV_DIR is the movement with direction (if known). Separate the cloud type entries from each other with a space. For example, a CB 21 nautical miles west of the observing location moving toward the east would be encoded "CB 21W MOV E." If a CB is more than 10 nautical miles to the west and distance cannot be determined, encode as "CB DSNT W." (2) **Towering cumulus** in format **TCU_[DIR]_[Plain Language]**, where TCU is cloud type and DIR is direction from the observing location. Separate the cloud type entries by a space. For example, a towering cumulus cloud up to 10 nautical miles west of the observing location would be encoded "TCU W." (3) **Altocumulus Castellanus** in format, **ACC_[DIR]_[Plain Language]**, where ACC is cloud type and DIR is direction from the observing location. Separate the cloud type entries by a space. For example, an ACC cloud 5 to 10 nautical miles northwest of the observing location would be encoded "ACC NW."	O			

Remark Number	Observed Condition	Enter in Remarks Section	Manual	Automated	Supplement	Back-up
19	Significant Cloud Types (cont)	(4) **Standing lenticular or Rotor clouds.** Stratocumulus (SCSL), altocumulus (ACSL), or cirrocumulus (CCSL), or rotor clouds in format, **CLD_[DIR]_[Plain Language]**, where CLD is cloud type and DIR is direction from the observing location. Separate the cloud type entries by a space. For example, ACSL clouds observed southwest through west of the observing location would be encoded "ACSL SW-W"; an apparent rotor cloud northeast of the observing location would be encoded "APRNT ROTOR CLD NE"; and CCSL clouds south of the observing location would be encoded "CCSL S."	O			
20	Ceiling Height at Second Location	Encode ceiling height at a second location in format, **CIG_hhh_[LOC]**, where CIG is the remark identifier, hhh is the measured height of the ceiling, and [LOC] is the specific location of the ceilometer(s) at the observing location. This remark is only generated when the ceiling is lower than that contained in the body of the report. For example, if the ceiling measured by a second sensor located at runway 11 is broken at 200 feet; the remark would be "CIG 002 RWY11."		X		
21	Pressure Rising or Falling Rapidly	Include **PRESRR** (pressure rising rapidly) or **PRESFR** (pressure falling rapidly) when the pressure is rising or falling at a rate of 0.06-inch Hg per hour or more, totaling a change 0.02-inch Hg or more at the time of observation,	X	X		X
22	Sea Level Pressure	Encode sea-level pressure in format **SLPppp**, where SLP is the remark identifier and ppp is the sea level pressure in hectopascals. For example, a sea level pressure of 998.2 hectopascals would be encoded as "SLP982." The FMQ-19 reports SLP on SPECI and METAR observations. If SLP is not available, it is encoded as "**SLPNO.**"	X	X		X
23	Aircraft Mishap	Include the remark **ACFT_MSHP_ [Plain Language]** to document weather conditions when notified of an aircraft mishap. The remark is not transmitted. Indicate non-transmission by enclosing the remark (ACFT MSHP) in parentheses in the observation.	X			X (see note 4)

Remark Number	Observed Condition	Enter in Remarks Section	Manual	Automated	Supplement	Back-up
24	**Snow Increasing Rapidly**	Include the snow increasing rapidly remark in the next METAR, whenever the snow depth increases by 1 inch or more in the past hour. Encode the remark in format, **SNINCR_[inches-hour/inches on ground]**, where SNINCR is the remark indicator, inches-hour is the depth increase in the past hour, and inches on ground is the total depth of snow on the ground at the time of the report. Separate the depth increase in the past hour and the total depth on the ground from each other by a solidus "/". For example, a snow depth increase of 2 inches in the past hour with a total depth on the ground of 10 inches would be encoded "SNINCR 2/10."	O			
25	**Other Significant Information** **[Plain Language Remarks]**	Added to report information significant to aircraft safety or resource protection. Amplifies entries in main observation. Some remarks will use the same order of entry as data the remark most closely relates (e.g., a VIS LWR E remark would have the entry as a sector visibility remark). (1) **Significant PIREP Information.** Any information from local PIREPs that may affect local flying operations, e.g., CLD LYR AT 400 FT ON APCH RWY 23 RPRTD BY PIREPS, CIG VIS LWR ON APCH RWY14L. (3) **Estimated Wind and Pressure. WND DATA ESTMD or ALSTG/SLP ESTMD** indicates the winds and/or pressure values from the primary airfield sensors are suspect or inoperative, and back-up equipment is being used. Do not estimate if using TMQ-53 as back-up and system has been sited properly. (4) **Significant Atmospheric Phenomena not Reported Elsewhere.** Present weather observed but not occurring at the point of observation or in the vicinity (e.g., SHRA OVR MTNS N). (6) **Aurora** observed in the past hour. Include **AURBO** in the next METAR and subsequent METARs throughout period of occurrence.	O ... X ... O ... O		O	X

Remark Number	Observed Condition	Enter in Remarks Section	Manual	Automated	Supplement	Back-up
25	Other Significant Information [Plain Language Remarks] (cont)	7) **Condensation Trails.** Include **CONTRAILS** to indicate condensation trails are observed. (8) **Location Unique Information** (as required), e.g., fog dispersal, rawinsonde data, state of ground, wind difference between parallel runways.	O O			
26	Hourly Precipitation Amount (METAR only)	Encode hourly precipitation amount in format, **Prrrr**, where P is the group indicator and rrrr is the water equivalent of all precipitation that has occurred since the last METAR. The amount is encoded in hundredths of an inch. For example, "P0009" would indicate 9/100 of an inch of precipitation fell in the past hour; "P0000" would indicate that less than 1/100 of an inch of precipitation fell in the past hour. Omit the group if no precipitation occurred since the last METAR.		X		O
27	3- and 6-Hour Precipitation Amount (See Note 2) (METAR only)	Encode the 3- and 6-hourly precipitation group in format, **6RRRR**, where 6 is the group indicator and RRRR is the amount of precipitation. Report the amount of precipitation (water equivalent) accumulated in the past 3 hours in the 3-hourly report; and the amount accumulated in the past 6 hours in the 6-hourly report. The amount of precipitation is encoded in inches, using the tens, units, tenths and hundredths digits of the amount. When an indeterminable amount of precipitation has occurred during the period, encode RRRR as 6////. For example, 2.17 inches of precipitation would be encoded "60217." A trace will be encoded "60000."	X	X		X
28	24-Hour Precipitation Amount (See Note 2) (METAR only)	Encode the 24-hour precipitation amount in format, $7R_{24}R_{24}R_{24}R_{24}$, where 7 is the group indicator and $R_{24}R_{24}R_{24}R_{24}$ is the 24-hour precipitation amount. Include the 24-hour precipitation amount in the 1200 UTC (or MAJCOM/Higher Headquarters designated time) whenever more than a trace of precipitation (water equivalent) has fallen in the preceding 24 hours. The amount of precipitation is encoded by using the tens, units, tenths, and hundredths of inches (water equivalent) for the 24-hour period. If more than a trace (water equivalent) has occurred and the amount cannot be determined, encode the group as 7////. For example, 1.25 inches of precipitation (water equivalent) in the past 24 hours will be encoded "70125."	X	X		O

Remark Number	Observed Condition	Enter in Remarks Section	Manual	Automated	Supplement	Back-up
29	**Snow Depth on Ground** (See Note 3) (METAR only)	Encode snow depth during normal airfield operating hours in the 0000, 0600, 1200, and 1800 UTC observation, or MAJCOM specified reporting time for your installation, when supplementing for snow depth. The remark is encoded in the format, **4/sss**, where 4/ is the group indicator and sss is the snow depth in whole inches using three digits. For example, a snow depth of 21 inches will be encoded as "4/021."	X(*)		X(*)	
30	**Hourly Temperature and Dew Point** (METAR only)	Encode the hourly temperature and dew point group to the tenth of a degree Celsius in format, $Ts_nT'T'T's_nT'_dT'_dT'_d$, where T is the group indicator, s_n is the sign of the temperature, T'T'T' is the temperature, and $T'_dT'_dT'_d$ is the dew point. Encode the sign of temperature and dew point as 1 if the value is below 0°C and 0 if the value is 0°C or higher. The temperature and dew point is reported in tens, units, and tenths of degrees Celsius. There will be no spaces between the entries. For example, a temperature of 2.6°C and dew point of -1.5°C would be reported in the body of the report as "03/M01" and the $Ts_nT'T'T's_nT'_dT'_dT'_d$ group as T00261015". If dew point is missing report the temperature; if the temperature is missing do not report the temperature/ dew point group.		X		O
31	**6-Hourly Maximum Temperature** (See Note 2) (METAR only)	Encode the 6-hourly maximum temperature group in format, $1s_nT_xT_xT_x$, where 1 is the group indicator, s_n is the sign of the temperature, $T_xT_xT_x$ is the maximum temperature in tenths of degrees Celsius using three digits. Encode the sign of maximum temperature as 1 if the maximum temperature is below 0°C and 0 if the maximum temperature is 0°C or higher. For example, a maximum temperature of -2.1°C would be encoded "11021"; 14.2°C would be encoded "10142."	O	X		O

Remark Number	Observed Condition	Enter in Remarks Section	Manual	Automated	Supplement	Back-up
32	**6-Hourly Minimum Temperature** (See Note 2) (METAR only)	Encode the 6-hourly minimum temperature group in format, $2s_nT_nT_nT_n$, where 2 is the group indicator, s_n is the sign of the temperature, and $T_nT_nT_n$ is the minimum temperature in tenths of degrees Celsius using three digits. Encode the sign of minimum temperature as 1 if the minimum temperature is below 0°C and 0 if the minimum temperature is 0°C or higher. For example, a minimum temperature of -0.1°C would be encoded "21001"; 1.2°C would be encoded "20012."	O	X		O
33	**24-Hour Maximum and Minimum Temperature** (METAR only)	Encode the 24-hour maximum temperature and the 24-hour minimum temperature in format, $4s_nT_xT_xT_xs_nT_nT_nT_n$, where 4 is the group indicator, s_n is the sign of the temperature, $T_xT_xT_x$ is the maximum 24-hour temperature, and TnTnTn is the 24-hour minimum temperature encoded in tenths of degrees Celsius using three digits. Encode the sign of maximum or minimum temperature as 1 if it is below 0°C and 0 if it is 0°C or higher. For example, a 24-hour maximum temperature of 10.0°C and a 24-hour minimum temperature of -1.5°C would be encoded "401001015"; a 24-hour maximum temperature of 11.2°C and a 24-hour minimum temperature of 8.4°C would be encoded as "401120084."		X		O
34	**3-Hourly Pressure Tendency** (See Note 2) (METAR only)	Encode the 3-hourly pressure tendency group in format, **5appp**, where 5 is the group indicator, "a" is the character of pressure change over the past 3 hours, and ppp is the amount of barometric change in tenths of hectopascals. The amount of barometric change is encoded using the tens, units, and tenths digits. For example, a steady increase of 3.2 hectopascals in the past three hours would be encoded "52032." **Note:** AMOSs report pressure net change code figures that **Table 12.2.** may not reflect, e.g., 001, 004, 006, 011.	O	X		O

Remark Number	Observed Condition	Enter in Remarks Section	Manual	Automated	Supplement	Back-up
35	Sensor Status Indicators	Report sensor outages using the following remarks: (1) **RVRNO** - Runway Visual Range information should be reported but is missing or not available. (2) **PWINO** - precipitation identifier information not available. (3) **PNO** - precipitation amount not available. (4) **FZRANO** - freezing rain information not available. (5) **TSNO** - thunderstorm information not available. (6) **VISNO (LOC)** - visibility at secondary location not available, e.g., VISNO RWY06. (7) **CHINO (LOC)** - (cloud-height-indicator) sky condition at secondary location not available, e.g., CHINO RWY06.	X	X X X X X X X		X
36	Maintenance Indicator	A maintenance indicator sign $ is appended at the end of the report when (e.g., AN/FMQ-19, ASOS) maintenance is needed on the system.		X		X

Remark Number	Observed Condition	Enter in Remarks Section	Manual	Automated	Supplement	Back-up
37	**(1) LAST** (manual EUs only)	(1) At limited-duty <u>manual EUs</u> and gunnery ranges, identify the last observation of the day (METAR or SPECI) by adding the term "LAST" following the last element in the observation text (e.g., TCU SE LAST).	X			
	(2) FIRST (See Note 2)	(2) The FIRST remark will be used to facilitate collection of observations from limited-duty EUs, and deployed <u>manual</u> EUs.	X			
	(3) COR	(3) Enter COR in column 13 followed by the time (to the nearest minute UTC) the correction was locally disseminated (e.g., COR 1426).	X		X	X

X - Indicates required data

* - See **Table 3.1**

O- Indicates optional based on local operational requirements

NOTES:
1. Encode at augmented EUs only if the initial SPECI taken for the beginning and/or ending of tornadic activity, thunderstorm, or hail was not transmitted longline, include the time of beginning (B) and/or ending (E) with the current (most recent) remark in the next SPECI or METAR observation transmitted longline. Enter the indicator B and/or E and the appropriate time(s) immediately following the phenomena reported (e.g., TSB35 12 SW MOV E, GR B37E39 GR 3/4). These B and/or E times are entered for longline transmission only.
2. Or as directed by MAJCOM or Higher Headquarters supplement for augmented EUs.
3. Or as directed by MAJCOM or Higher Headquarters supplement for augmented and automated EUs.
4. Encode "Aircraft Mishap" when an aircraft mishap occurs while operating in a back-up mode.

Attachment 4

STATION INFORMATION

Required Information in the Station Information File

STATION INFORMATION FILE	
Physical Characteristics	- Name of Installation. - Station ICAO Identifier. - WMO Index Number. - Time Zone (+/- relative to UTC). - Latitude/Longitude to the nearest minute - Field Elevation. - Station Elevation (or elevation of AMOS, primary group). - Elevation of Primary Barometer (or elevation of AMOS, primary group).
Observing Operation (consistent with FLIP entires)	- Full automated operations (provide operating hours). - Augmented observations (provide hours observations are available).
Sensor Data	- AMOS. Date installed and commissioned. - Location of AMOS sensors in relation to the airfield runways. - Legacy Fixed-Base Sensors (list all). - Location of legacy sensors in relation to the airfield runways. - Explain any non-standard siting of sensors. - Provide listing of AMOS back-up equipment.
Physical Description of Observation Site.	Include additional features that affect the weather or climatology. For example, surrounding surface grass, dirt, concrete, asphalt, nearby bodies of water, trees/forest, etc. Include available maps, layouts, photos, etc.